CAFÉ LOGOS YEAR C

A COMPREHENSIVE AND EXCITING NEW RESOURCE FOR 11-16 YEAR OLDS

PETE TOWNSEND

First published in 2000 by
KEVIN MAYHEW LTD
Buxhall
Stowmarket
Suffolk IP14 3BW

0 1 2 3 4 5 6 7 8 9

ISBN 1 84003 620 6
Catalogue No. 1500383

Cover design by Jaquetta Sergeant
Edited by Helen Elliot
Typesetting by Richard Weaver
Printed and bound in Great Britain

CONTENTS

ACKNOWLEDGEMENTS

There is a great deal of satisfaction in putting the last full stop at the end of the last sentence on the last page of the book. I've lost count of the number of full stops on the pages of this book and I've also lost count of the number of 'full stops' I've reached when inspiration is no more than a dream and the next sentence is nothing more than wishful thinking. It's at these times that I'm ever grateful for the support and encouragement of my family and friends.

Thanks to Helen and Liz for being there. To Ed and Jane for listening ears. To Nig and Carol for always being willing to pick up from where we left off. Billy, Shaz and their artistic impressions: never argue with a coelacanth riding a motorbike! And to Dale, Nathan, Esme and Laurie for the empty crisp packets that decorate the kitchen. Most of all to Ruth for sharing a life.

INTRODUCTION

Hello! Welcome back to Café Logos. Glad to see you again. For those of you visiting for the first time, take a seat and peruse the menu. You'll find a feast of ideas to entertain, challenge and tickle your sense buds.

The menu is based on the Common Worship Lectionary, Year C. The inspiration for the Café is found in Psalm 34, 'taste and see that the Lord is good' and in 1 Peter 2:1-12, 'a living stone'. The idea is to identify with Jesus as the Living Stone by discussion ('taste and see') and to explore a faith in Jesus through the use of the 'Logos' (God's living message).

Each week is identified as a 'unit'. Units 1-24 are based on the Gospels and explore the life of Jesus. Units 25-42 look at the Epistles and examine the Christian life, while Units 43-48 relate to the Psalms and take a closer look at how being a Christian can affect our daily lives.

All of the main Church calendar events are covered with lots of extra material for you to insert between 'events'. Unit 1 correlates to the beginning of the Lectionary year. However, if you want to start using *Café Logos* before then, simply use some of the later units (namely 33-43). You can identify which units to use by checking with the index of themes.

The menu is divided into six sections, with icons for easy recognition.

TODAY'S SPECIAL: theme and Bible reading for the day.

Nibbles: activities which focus the group on the day's theme.

Tasty bit: an introduction and link to the teaching, using suggestions for worship songs and drama.

Chewy bit: the main teaching session with ideas and guidelines for sharing.

Munchy bit: discussion, thought and focus.

Afters: prayer, reflection and ideas for sharing.

The references to worship songs are only suggestions. You can substitute other material on a similar theme if you prefer. You can either use the worship songs as part of group worship or use the lyrics in discussion. All of the worship suggestions can be found in *The source* (Kevin Mayhew 1998), *The source new songs* (Kevin Mayhew 1999), *World Wide Worship No. 1* (Kevin Mayhew 1999) and *Re:source 2000* (Kevin Mayhew 1999).

The drama material is intentionally kept simple, needing only basic props and two actors. This requires little preparation time and the script can be attached to clipboards, placed on the floor or stuck onto props so that you can ad lib to your heart's content. Have fun, enjoy the menu and taste and see that the Lord is good!

If you've any comments or suggestions I'd love to hear from you. Contact me at: townie@postmaster.co.uk

TODAY'S SPECIAL

Pay attention at the back!

Luke 21:25-36: When the Son of Man appears

Equipment:
child's short story book
bag of sweets
small squares of paper
music and lyrics

As each member of the group arrives, give them a square of paper which has a number written on it. (Don't make it easy. Have numbers such as 1927, 6749 or 5463.) Don't tell anyone what the numbers mean. Begin to read the story. Try and use a boring voice which drones on and on. At intervals, drop one of the numbers into a sentence, for example 'And when Jack fell down the 6749'. If the person with the number responds, give them a sweet. Every second or third number, refuse to give the person a sweet even if they respond on hearing their number. Make the numbers and giving out sweets as random as possible so that none of the group are sure whether a response will earn them a sweet or not.

(Allow ten minutes for this activity.)

Expectations, disappointment, frustration? These are all common feelings when things happen or don't happen as we expect them to.

Have a look at 'I've set my heart on you' by Stephen Hamilton (*Re:source 2000*, 5) or 'Be patient, be ready' by Graham Kendrick (*The source*, 46).

(Allow approximately five minutes.)

Ask the group what they thought of the lyrics for the chosen song. What point were the lyrics trying to make?

Read Luke 21:25-36.

It doesn't seem as if a week goes by without reports of something happening in the sky, news of tidal waves or treacherous storms at sea, or even the threat of asteroids hitting the earth! Earthquakes, tornadoes, flash floods cause many people to be frightened and panic. There is a problem. Weather forecasts and predictions try to warn us of what may happen, but if they are so accurate, why do so many people get caught out?

Guessing what the weather will do can be a tricky business. It's no joke walking in a crowd of people when you're dressed in waterproof coat, wellington boots, plastic bags wrapped around your legs and a bucket on your head, and everybody else is wearing short sleeves and sunglasses. So, you ignore the weather forecast of torrential rain, go out in short sleeves and sunglasses and promptly get soaked. Sometimes you just can't win.

But, let's be honest, most of us would prefer to know what to expect rather than be kept guessing. Some surprises are OK, such as a birthday or Christmas, provided you've given everyone enough hints.

In the Bible reading, Jesus said that there would be lots of warnings and signs about his return but no one will know for sure when it's going to happen. Some of the things that Jesus referred to happen very frequently, almost too frequently. For instance, people in San Francisco, America, know they live in a major earthquake area. Earthquakes have happened before and occasionally earth tremors hint at what may be to come. But no one knows exactly when 'the big one' will happen. They prepare for it, they rehearse possible scenarios and plan how they may react to a major earthquake. But still no one knows when.

Even if you know it's going to happen sometime, isn't it possible that you can become a bit bored with wondering when it's going to happen? Rather like having a fire drill – the alarm sounds and you evacuate the building . . . eventually. Well, it's only a rehearsal, isn't it?

In San Francisco, they know history is going to repeat itself and another major earthquake will hit the city. They can't live every day in fear and they can't live every day ignoring the evidence. They watch, wait and prepare. Pretty much just what Jesus asks of us.

Give each member of the group a piece of card. Ask them to spend a few moments thinking about issues that concern them. It may be personal, local, national or international. For instance: political unrest, homelessness, poverty, victims of natural disasters or the environment. Ask them to write the issue/s on the card and place the cards on a notice board. Personal issues can be kept private by just having a name or topic written on the card. Try and keep the notice board up to date and use as a focal point for prayer and quiet moments of reflection.

(Allow five minutes.)

Suggest that the group spend a few moments considering the issues on the notice board. While everyone is quiet, read the following verses from Psalm 16:

Protect me, Lord God! I run to you for safety,
  and I have said, 'Only you are my Lord!
Every good thing I have is a gift from you.'

You, Lord, are all I want!
You are my choice, and you keep me safe.
You make my life pleasant, and my future is bright.
I praise you Lord, for being my guide.
Even in the darkest night,
  your teachings fill my mind.
I will always look to you,
  as you stand beside me and protect me from fear.

TODAY'S SPECIAL

Under the thumb?

Luke 3:1-6: The preaching of John the Baptist

Equipment:
bag of doughnuts
rubber bands
candle
music and lyrics or drama sketch

Tie the rubber bands together so that you have a rubber 'rope' about a metre long. Attach the 'rope' to the doughnut. Ask the group to form pairs. While one of the pair is lying on their back, the second person stands on a chair and attempts to 'feed' the doughnut to their partner by bouncing the doughnut towards their partner's mouth. The person lying on the floor is not allowed to move or lift their head at any time. If you're feeling 'kind' the person feeding their partner can bounce the doughnut with their hand. If you want to add a good dose of fun, get the 'feeder' to hold the rubber 'rope' between their teeth and then attempt to feed their partner. It's not compulsory, but you might like to have something to help the person being fed to clean themselves afterwards.

(Allow ten minutes for this activity.)

It can be really frustrating when what you want is almost within reach. It can be equally frustrating for the person holding what they know you want when they can't succeed in satisfying your need. Have a look at 'Open the eyes of my heart' by Paul Baloche (*The source new songs*, 49) or 'Come, let us return' by Graham Kendrick (*The source* 72). Alternatively, you might like to use the drama sketch *The Wrinklies at the park* (see page 15).

(Allow approximately five minutes.)

Read Luke 3:1-6.

Verses 4-6 of this reading are taken from Isaiah 40:3-5. These words were spoken to the people of Israel while they were exiled in Babylon. Exile meant that they were far from home and that many of the young Israelites were born in exile and didn't know anything other than the land of their exile.

Exile also meant living as captives: never knowing freedom. The ability of the Israelites to promote their culture and traditions was severely limited. They couldn't live as they wanted to or behave in any way that might annoy their captors. They would often be made to work in situations that were at best unpleasant and at worst so bad they'd reduce their life expectancy to zero! The exiles' lives were not their own; they belonged, body and soul, to their captors.

The words in verses 4-6 announce the end of captivity and the start of a new life of freedom.

At the time of John the Baptist, Galilee and Judea were under Roman rule. Although the people weren't physically in exile they were captives in their own land. The Romans brought with them traditions, customs, beliefs, politics and a lifestyle that were distinctly 'foreign'. No wonder that John the Baptist's words were greeted with such enthusiasm. Most of the people wanted an end to the Roman occupation and were fed up with being 'exiles' in their own land.

However, John was referring to the people's emotional and spiritual exile. It was an exile that had seen the people become so busy with customs and traditions that they had gradually lost sight of who God was. The people had become captives of a society that presented many alternatives to God and as many ways to God as there were roads to Rome.

John announced the coming of 'one' who would 'straighten the crooked paths and smooth out the rough roads' (verse 5). John was preparing the way for the people to return to God and know what it was to be where they belonged, no longer captives to fear, suffering and death, allowing their lives to be cared for and guided by the Heavenly Father.

Ask the group how they felt about the activity in the 'tasty bit'. Did they feel annoyed, or frustrated at being unable to eat the doughnut or even angry at the mess they got into? Do they think that God may feel like this at times? Especially when he sees the people he cares for get physically or emotionally hurt, frustrated with life or facing rejection?

If they were in God's place, what would they do?

(Allow five minutes.)

Place a lighted candle in the middle of the room. Ask the group to look at the flame and think of this as representing Jesus. He gave his life to a world that was captive to a way of life that kept them away from God.

After a few moments, read the following prayer:

Lord, it feels, at times,
   that I'm walking through treacle.
Each step takes so much effort,
   and I know,
   that the next time I put my foot down
   it's going to be messy . . . again.
I want to follow you,
   but when the going gets tough
   my feet get stuck.
It wouldn't be so much of a problem
   if everything was OK here, right now.
But, well, it's sort of sticky, you know how it is.
What with this and that,
   that and this,
   and plenty of bother.
I think I need you, Lord,
   to help me out.
Providing you've got
   a bucket of hot soapy water,
   scrubbing brush and a towel.

THE WRINKLIES AT THE PARK

Characters	Two wrinkled grumps who like nothing better than to have a whinge about anything and everything.
Scene	The two Wrinklies sitting on a park bench watching all the people passing by on their way to hear John the Baptist.
Props	two old raincoats hats walking stick umbrella park bench pair of tatty sandals for Old 1

Old 1 Gracious me, would you just look at that!

Old 2 What's that, then?

Old 1 Over there, look. *(Points into distance)*

Old 2 *(Rubs eyes and stares into distance)* What?

Old 1 Are you blind or summat?

Old 2 Nah, just takes me eyes a few moments to get adjusted, that's all. Now, what are you on about?

Old 1 Her over there *(points)* see?

Old 2 *(Nods head)* Oh her. Haven't seen her about for a while. Last I heard she'd taken to her bed after a drop too much of the falling-over juice.

Old 1 *(Cackles)* Must be summat good to get her out of bed.

Old 2 Usually a jumble sale. Haven't heard of one, have you?

Old 1 Nah, *(waves sandals under nose of Old 2)* got these last time. They've seen a few sights.

Old 2 *(Holds nose)* Smells like they've stepped in a few as well.

Old 1 It's them donkeys. Don't care where they do their business. You'd think the authorities would do summat about it. Pays me taxes, regular.

Old 2 Don't give me authorities. Right bunch of parasites. It's all take, take, take.

Old 1 Too right. As long as they're all right, nothing and nobody else matters.

Old 2 It's about time somebody stood up to them. Told 'em a few things, put 'em straight. *(Waves walking stick in the air)* If I were a few years younger, I'd make them see sense, good smack around the head, that's what they need.

Old 1 Steady on, who's rattled your cage?

Old 2 Well, it ain't right.

Old 1 What ain't?

Old 2 Anything you care to think of.

Old 1 Got out of bed the wrong side, eh?

Old 2 Wasn't worth going to bed. Couldn't sleep.

Old 1 Your old trouble playing up again?

Old 2 *(Looks at knees)* Nah, they're all right. It's all those folk walking past my house.

Old 1 What they up to, then?

Old 2 They're traipsing off to see that weird bloke, you know, the one who keeps shouting his mouth off about getting ready for summat or other.

Old 1	Who, Zec and Liz's lad?
Old 2	That's the one. Been living in the desert, so I hear.
Old 1	That's not all I've heard.
Old 2	*(Nudges Old 1)* Go on, what have you heard? I enjoy a bit of gossip. D'ya hear about old Ben and that mix up with the goat's cheese?
Old 1	What was that, then?
Old 2	Turns out he'd been milking old Joe's goats at night, making the cheese and selling it.
Old 1	Didn't Joe think summat was wrong when he didn't get any milk from his goats?
Old 2	Nah, he just thought the goats had run dry. He spent a fortune in vets' bills.
Old 1	What did old Ben say when he got caught?
Old 2	He reckoned the goats were wild and anyone could have milked 'em.
Old 1	Were they running wild?
Old 2	Nah, they were in Joe's back yard.
Old 1	What's old Ben like, eh?
Old 2	Well, at least he dresses properly, not like that fella in the desert. All dressed up in camel hair.
Old 1	Bit itchy.
Old 2	Doesn't seem to bother him. Reckons the only thing that bothers him is all the bad things people have done and that they should turn back to God.

Old 1 Who does he think he is?

Old 2 Well, he's said to be the creator and . . .

Old 1 Not God, you dozy lump, this desert fella.

Old 2 Oh, John they call him, John the Baptist.

Old 1 The Baptist?

Old 2 Yeah, tells people they're dirty inside and throws 'em in the river.

Old 1 Don't think I'd want to swallow much of that River Jordan; too many people wash their feet in there, including you.

Old 2 I'll ignore that. Anyway, this John fella caused a bit of a stir when those Pharisees and Sadducees went up to see him.

Old 1 What did he do?

Old 2 Called 'em a load of snakes.

Old 1 Bet that rattled 'em!

Old 2 He wants to be careful what he says, could get himself into trouble saying the wrong things. *(Stands up)* Right, I'm off then.

Old 1 Me too. Gonna go and see this John fella. I reckon my feet could do with a wash.

TODAY'S SPECIAL

Turning on the heat

Luke 3:7-18: The message of John the Baptist

Equipment:
plastic carrier bag
music and lyrics

Welcome the group as normal but – your appearance is far from normal!

Make sure that you are only dressed in a pair of shorts and a ripped T-shirt. Once the group have sat down and given you some odd looks, apologise for the way you are dressed (or not!). Explain that you have had a bad time and all you have left in the world is what they see. Don't offer any explanation for your 'loss'.

Pick up the plastic carrier bag and hold it out in front of you. With a sad expression on your face, politely ask the group if any of them would be willing to give you some essential items such as socks, shoes, jumper, coat. Place any(!) donated items in the bag.

(Allow ten minutes for this activity.)

Does someone's 'odd' behaviour make you feel uncomfortable? How do we react to expressions of eccentric behaviour?

See what you think of 'These are the days' by Robin Mark (*Re:source 2000*, 14) or 'The Spirit of the Lord' by Graham Kendrick (*Re:source 2000*, 15).

(Allow approximately five minutes.)

Ask the group what they thought of your behaviour. Did it embarrass them? Or did they think it was a funny stunt? Would they have responded differently if it had been real?

Read Luke 3:7-18.

You have to imagine the scene: out of the desert comes this large, hairy man, dressed in clothes made of camel's hair, a leather strap around his waist and living on a diet of grasshoppers and wild honey (see Matthew 3:4). Not only does he look a tiny bit different, but he's shouting his head off about all manner of things!

After quoting the prophet Isaiah, John then goes on to call a load of people 'snakes who come running from judgement'.

John had spent a long time in the desert, some might say too long! The desert was covered in brushwood, twigs and dry stalks of dead plants. At times a spark could set the desert alight, burning anything that could be burnt. When this happened, it was common for vipers to slither out of the nooks and crannies where they lay hidden, and attempt to escape the flames. It was this picture that John must have had in his head when the people rushed to hear what he had to say. Some thought he was the Messiah, a claim he quickly denied by saying that he was not good enough to untie the sandals of the one to come. (The act of undoing someone's sandals was the act of a servant.)

The people who came to John wanted to know what they had to do to escape the 'coming judgement' (see verse 7). John didn't tell them to get down and pray, go to church as often as they could or read the scripture continuously; he directed his comments at their lifestyle. John told the tax collectors not to overcharge to line their own pockets, he told the soldiers not to charge protection money and he told those who were well-off to share what they had with the poor. These were all issues that Jesus later tackled.

John was trying to make it clear that just appearing to act 'godly', by going to church, reading the Bible and praying, was not what God required. God wanted a change of heart which would be reflected by the way people lived.

What do the group think about the way that John spoke to the people who came to see him? Wasn't he making enemies rather than encouraging people to turn back to God and be baptised (verse 3)? Eventually, John did use a few too many words when he criticised Herod Antipas, ruler of the area, for marrying Herodias (who was, at one time, Herod's sister-in-law and his niece). Herod Antipas met Herodias, who was married to another bloke called . . . Herod. He seduced her and later married her. Now, Herod Antipas was related to Herod who was married to Herodias (!) In one way and another, Herod, Herod Antipas and Herodias were all related through Herod the Great. It gets confusing (not to mention a severe lack of imagination when it comes to names), but by the standards of Jewish law and opinion the marriage of Herod Antipas and Herodias was well out of order. Using a few choice words, John the Baptist pointed out that Herod Antipas' actions were wrong, which resulted in John being shoved in prison for his failure to compromise his message.

Are there any areas of our lives where John's lack of compromise would embarrass us?

Ask the group to consider areas of their lives about which John might have a few choice words to say. While the group think about these issues, ask them to imagine God asking them to turn their backs on these areas and walk away, with the confidence of having God's arm around their shoulders.

After a period of quiet, read Psalm 25:1-10:

I offer you my heart, Lord God, and I trust you.
Don't make me ashamed or let enemies defeat me.
Don't disappoint any of your worshippers,
  but disappoint all deceitful liars.
Show me your paths and teach me to follow;
  guide me by your truth and instruct me.
You keep me safe, and I always trust you.

Please, Lord, remember,
  you have always been patient and kind.
Forget each wrong I did when I was young.
Show how truly kind you are and remember me.
You are honest and merciful,
  and you teach sinners how to follow your path.
You lead humble people to do what is right
  and to stay on your path.
In everything you do, you are kind and faithful
  to everyone who keeps our agreement with you.

TODAY'S SPECIAL

Ordinarily extraordinary

Luke 1:39-45: Mary visits Elizabeth

Equipment:
postcards
music and lyrics
large sheet of paper

Write one of the statements below on each postcard.

1. A giraffe can clean its ears with its 52-centimetre tongue.
2. Fingernails grow nearly four times faster than toenails.
3. Clinophobia is the fear of beds.
4. A mole can dig a 100-metre tunnel in just one night.
5. Slugs have four noses.
6. A sneeze travels out of your nose at over 100 miles per hour.
7. The elephant is the only mammal that can't jump.
8. More *Monopoly* money is printed in a year than real money.
9. More people use blue toothbrushes than red ones.
10. No piece of paper can be folded in half more than seven times.

Give the cards to group members and ask them to read the statement on the card. They can then ask the rest of the group whether they think the statement is true or false. (All the statements are true . . . check them out!)

(Allow 10 minutes for this activity.)

Some statements just seem far too weird to be true. Some facts can be proven, some can be disproved and others we may never understand.

Take a look at 'You have taken the precious' by Kevin Prosch and Tom Davis (*The source*, 600) or 'From heaven you came' by Graham Kendrick (*The source*, 114).

(Allow approximately 5 minutes.)

What did the group think about the lyrics of the chosen song? Are there statements that take a bit of thinking about or seem too difficult to take in?

Read Luke 1:39-45.

Most people are really pleased when someone tells them about an eagerly awaited pregnancy. There's weeks of planning and preparation, every conversation seems to be centred around the coming event and it's hard to think about anything else (especially if you're the parents!).

It's much the same for an unplanned pregnancy, except that the conversation isn't always too encouraging! In fact, the conversation, or gossip, isn't always very complimentary.

You can imagine how Mary felt. Here she was, a teenager, engaged to a respectable bloke and along pops an angel to tell her she's pregnant. It didn't help matters that she came from an area that had a bit of a rough reputation to start with. Mary came from Nazareth, which was considered to be a no-go area for any respectable Jew. Nazareth was full of non-Jews (and some Jews) who didn't observe all the requirements of the Jewish law. Nazareth also attracted 'foreigners' who brought with them customs and traditions that were thought to be a bit dodgy for Jews.

So, after discovering that she is pregnant, Mary goes off to another town to visit her cousin Elizabeth. Elizabeth's husband is a priest and is respected in his community. Elizabeth opens the door and immediately Mary greets her with the news that she's engaged to Joseph (how nice for you, dear!), she's a virgin (Joseph will be pleased) and she's pregnant (Joseph will definitely not be pleased).

You would imagine Elizabeth would be shocked but she isn't! Instead her baby (to be born John the Baptist) moves in her womb and Elizabeth celebrates the news!

Elizabeth isn't a stranger to the unusual. She and her husband, Zechariah, were both harvesting wrinkles (getting old) and didn't have any children, and this in a society that considered children a blessing and to be without children a punishment from God.

Put simply, Zechariah moaned to God about not having children, God sent an angel to tell Zechariah that Elizabeth would have a son, Elizabeth became pregnant, Zechariah moaned to God (who said 'typical man'?), and God caused Zechariah to be dumb (lucky Elizabeth) until the birth of John.

Because of her own situation, Elizabeth was able to understand what Mary was going through and called her 'fortunate' because Mary chose to believe God. Both Elizabeth and Mary chose to believe and trust in God in situations that were far from normal.

Ask the group to imagine how Zechariah might have reacted to Mary's news. He is a respected member of the community and his wife's cousin arrives with some disturbing news. Could he have thought: 'Well, what do you expect, coming from Nazareth?' or 'What are the other priests going to say about this?'

How do we react to news that's a little hard to believe or is something we don't really want to hear? Do we dismiss it straightaway or think for a few seconds and then dismiss it?

(Allow 5 minutes.)

Place a large sheet of paper on the wall. Draw a large question mark on the paper. Ask the group to look at the question mark. Ask them whether they treat information or situations that they don't understand as untrue or wrong purely because they cannot relate to what they're hearing.

Ask everyone to spend a few moments in reflection while you read the following Bible verses:

Psalm 86:11-13.
Teach me to follow you, and I will obey your truth.
Always keep me faithful.
With all my heart I thank you.
I praise you, Lord God.
Your love for me is so great
 that you protect me from death and the grave.

TODAY'S SPECIAL

Including you!

Luke 2:41-52: The boy Jesus in the temple

Equipment:
postcards
paper and pens
envelopes
music and lyrics

On the postcards write the following categories:

Short	Tall
Rabbit	Chicken
Stream	Pond
Athlete	Singer
Coffee	Tea
Porsche	Land-Rover

Divide the group in two and ask them to choose which of the categories they would like to be. For instance, if the categories chosen are 'Rabbit' and 'Chicken' then one half of the group will be rabbits and the other half chickens. You may need to 'help' the groups decide who is to be either the rabbit or the chicken. Give each group a sheet of paper and a pen and ask them to write down a list of qualities for their word. What are the benefits of being a rabbit? What's good about being a chicken?

Ask one member of each group to read their group's list of qualities and the other group can offer reasons why it is better to be in the other category.

Repeat the process with the other categories.

(Allow 10 minutes for this activity.)

What criteria do we use to make the kind of judgements that were made in the previous activity?

Have a look at 'When the music fades' by Matt Redman (*Re:source 2000*, 16) or 'Lord, you have my heart' by Martin Smith (*The source*, 341).

(Allow approximately 5 minutes.)

What did the group think the lyrics of the song were attempting to say?

Read Luke 2:41-52.
Before we start to think about this account, by Luke, of Jesus getting himself into grief with his parents, it's worth trying to understand a little of the background.

At the age of 12, a Jewish boy officially becomes a man and takes on the associated duties and obligations. Jesus and his parents had travelled to Jerusalem to attend his first Passover (a meal to commemorate the exodus of the Israelites from captivity in Egypt). When it was time to go home, the women would have travelled together and set out earlier than the men. The men would follow later and both parties would meet up at the evening camp. You can imagine that both Mary and Joseph thought Jesus was travelling with the other parent: 'I thought he was with you!' 'No, I thought he was with you!'

Eventually, Jesus was found in the temple where the Sanhedrin (the supreme Jewish court) was meeting in public to discuss religious and theological questions. After three days' search, Mary and Joseph found Jesus listening to the discussions and asking questions. It was significant that at the same time as he reached adulthood, Jesus also acknowledged who he was and who his father was (see verse 49).

Jesus became aware of his status as an adult and the value that God placed upon him. It was this knowledge that gave him the motivation to return home with his parents, continue to learn the trade of a carpenter and allow his future to remain secure in God's hands.

Give each member of the group a pen, some paper and an envelope. Ask them how they would have felt if they'd been made aware that they had a special purpose, something that would make a real difference in the world? Would they have been eager to get 'on with it' or would they keep their head down and hope it all went away?

Do any of the group feel that they have a talent or gift for something that excites them or encourages them to dream about their future? Suggest to the group that they should write their 'dream' down on the piece of paper. Below, ask them to write down some ideas about how they can achieve that 'dream'. When complete, fold the paper and place it in the envelope and seal it closed. Offer to keep the envelopes in a secure place (promise not to peep) and they can open the envelope in twelve months' time and see if they think the same and whether they've made any progress towards their 'dream'.

Encourage each member of the group to understand that each one of them is special and God wants the best for them.

(Allow 5 minutes.)

Once the group have given you the sealed envelopes, place them in a central place and ask the group to be quiet while you read the following prayer:

Lord, I know,
  no matter how I feel right now,
  whether it's a dustbin or a toilet,
  you see us for who we really are –
  precious people who you care for, every day.
It's difficult, I mean really difficult,
  to see above the mess and clutter
  that surrounds us.
I'm glad that you can see through the rubbish
  and look at my life with love.
Help me
  to trust,
  to see,
  to feel
  your love,
  no matter what I feel like. Amen.

TODAY'S SPECIAL

In the neighbourhood!

John 1:10-18: The Word of life

Equipment:
postcards (sufficient for most members of the group to take part in the game)
paper and pens
music and lyrics

Each of the postcards should have a word on with two or three different definitions. This is a kind of biblical *Call My Bluff.* For example:

SPIKENARD

Definition 1. During Old Testament times, people would travel around by riding on a donkey. When the travellers reached their destination they would tie the donkey to a special post which was usually found at the rear of a house. The word *Spikenard* was the name given to this type of post.

Definition 2. In biblical times people didn't wash their hair as often as we do today. Rather than allow their hair to look or smell unclean, people would use a perfume, *Spikenard,* to comb through their hair.
(Correct definition.)

MIZPAH

Definition 1. When guests visited unexpectedly, the host would offer a small cake with some wine. The cake, or *Mizpah*, was similar to a mini-doughnut and flavoured with honey.

Definition 2. In Old Testament times it was important always to be on the lookout for thieves or potential enemies who might attempt to sneak up and attack a village or encampment. A tower would be built to provide a look-out point. Such a tower is called a *Mizpah*.
(Correct definition.)

You can write other zany definitions using a Bible dictionary with a large dose of imagination. Divide the group into teams and give each team a selection of words. Each player reads out a definition and the other team have to decide which is the correct definition.

(Allow 10 minutes for this activity.)

Some things we find difficult to understand. And sometimes it's not the understanding that's important but being thankful. Have a look at 'God is here' by Ian Smale (*The source*, 127) or 'What a friend I've found' by Martin Smith (*The source*, 565).

(Allow approximately 5 minutes.)

What is the point of having friends? Ask the group how they would define friendship.

Read John 1:10-18.
If you ever get around to reading the book of Proverbs, in the Old Testament, you will find loads of comments about friendship. One in particular has a neat way of putting across the value of friends:

'The sweet smell of incense can make you feel good, but true friendship is better still' (Proverbs 27:9).

In other words, a temporary pleasant smell can surround us and be pleasing and possibly disguise some bad odours (!) but it doesn't last. A real friend is someone who hangs around even when things don't look or smell too clever. You can easily find out who your real friends are – by the time you've finished spelling the word 'trouble' see how many of your supposed friends are left standing next to you.

The song 'What a friend I've found' has one line which says: 'What a friend I've found, closer than a brother'. That's some statement to make.

In John's Gospel we can find a similar awesome statement. In verse 14 of the reading, John writes that:

'The Word became a human being and lived here with us.'

John the Baptist was saying that Jesus was God's spoken Word, the Word which gives light and life, and that God chose, through Jesus, to come and live with us.

The original word used in John's Gospel for 'live' is 'tabernacle' which literally means 'putting a tent up'. A tent isn't usually a permanent place to live. John the Baptist understood that Jesus was only going to be 'living' with them for a short time (33 years from birth to crucifixion). But the message that Jesus brought was that he now wanted to come and live with us permanently, to become a part of us, to share our every experience and be with us every step of every day.

Jesus doesn't just want to move into the neighbourhood, or even move in next door, he wants to become an essential part of our life, a central part of our existence.

Ask the group what they think a friend is.

- What qualities does someone need to be called a friend?
- Are there any limits to what a friend should know about you?
- Is it important to keep some areas of our life private?
- Does having a close friend make us feel vulnerable, insecure or leave us open to having a supposed friend gossip about us?

Write down some of the details that the group agree are essential qualities for a friend. You might like to include some of the ways which the group think a friend shouldn't behave.

(Allow 5 minutes.)

Suggest to the group that they stay quiet as you read an extract from the following Psalm. The group might like to look at some of the 'qualities' a friend needs.

Psalm 139:1-6.
You have looked deep into my heart, Lord,
  and you know all about me.
You know when I am resting or when I am working,
  and from heaven you discover my thoughts.

You notice everything I do and everywhere I go.
Before I even speak a word,
  you know what I will say,
  and with your powerful arm
  you protect me from every side.
I can't understand this!
Such wonderful knowledge is far above me.

TODAY'S SPECIAL

Awesome!

Matthew 2:1-12: The wise men

Equipment:
flipchart
cards
pen
music and lyrics

Arrange for one of the group to act as your assistant for this activity. You will need to have a quick rehearsal before you attempt this experiment in artificial stupidity!

Ask one of the group to think of a number between one and ten. That member of the group then whispers the number to your 'assistant'. Announce to the group that you will now tell them what the number is.

Ask your assistant to sit down on a chair. Place your hands on the assistant's head with your thumbs on their jaw, just below their ears. Ask your assistant to concentrate on the number they were given. While they are doing this, you must look around the room and stare for a few seconds at any object, then move on to stare at something else. As you are doing this, your assistant should clench his/her teeth together the number of times that corresponds to the number chosen. When you have finished counting, suddenly smack your hands together (preferably after removing them from your assistant's head) and tell the rest of the group the number.

Perform this as often as you wish or until someone guesses how you're doing it!

(Allow 10 minutes for this activity.)

We all enjoy being amazed by things we don't understand. It's even more fun trying to guess how a trick was worked or how somebody achieved something.

Take a look at 'I fall down' by Shonelle Barnes (*Re:source 2000*, 3) or 'I could sing unending songs' by Martin Smith (*The source*, 200).

(Allow approximately 5 minutes.)

Ask the group what they thought about the lyrics. Did they make any kind of sense?

Read Matthew 2:1-12.
Every Christmas we see them, dressed in dressing gowns and wearing paper crowns. The three 'wise men' take their tinsel-covered shoe boxes and present them to the plastic doll lying in the cot. Everybody sighs at the little boy dressed as a donkey and laughs at the two girls fighting with the black-and-white sheet that allows them to pretend they are a cow. It's all part of the Christmas story. It's familiar, safe and we wouldn't feel the same without it.

What's that got to do with 'awesome'? Take the three 'wise men'. These 'wise men' or magi, were religious leaders and scholars from an area we now know as Iran and the surrounding countries. We always think of them as being only three, but there were more than likely up to a hundred of them travelling together (we think of three wise men because of the three gifts).

The magi travelled a huge distance, covering mountains and desert, through storms and possible encounters with bandits along the way. We are told they followed a 'star' which came to rest over Bethlehem. Chinese astronomers recorded a comet around 5 BC which travelled slowly across the sky and its 'tail' pointed towards Bethlehem. This comet became visible on the first day of the Egyptian month Mesori. Mesori literally means 'birth of a prince'. With this knowledge, the magi set off on a long and hazardous journey to see who this prince could be.

The magi walked away from everything that was safe and familiar so that they could find this special child and offer their worship. They brought with them the three gifts that would signify the role of the child: gold for royalty; frankincense for priesthood and myrrh for death.

For the magi to leave their homes and travel over rough terrain and face unknown dangers so that they could see the infant Jesus, that's awesome.

Have a flipchart and marker pen ready. Ask the group to define the word 'awesome'.

- What does it mean to them?
- Have they any examples of something which they consider to be awesome?
- Have they done something which they, or others, think was an awesome thing to do?

- Do they have an idea or an ambition which they believe it would be awesome to achieve?
- What do they need to do to achieve that ambition?
- To what lengths would they go to achieve that ambition?

(Allow 5 minutes.)

Have seven large cards available. On each card write one letter from the word 'awesome'. Place the first card on the flipchart and ask the group to think about their dreams and ambitions. While they are thinking, turn the card over to reveal the word: 'Almighty'. Do this with each of the other cards.

A: Almighty
W: Wonderful
E: Everlasting
S: Saviour
O: Omnipotent
M: Majestic
E: Everywhere

After you have revealed each of the words and the group have recognised each one as telling us a little bit about God's character, finish with the following prayer:

God, you are
Almighty, creator of all things seen and unseen.
You are Wonderful, absolutely amazing, totally astounding.
You are Everlasting in your love for each one of us.
You are our Saviour, our rescuer from everything
that would try and put a barrier between us.
You are Omnipotent, powerful, able to do the
impossible, able to love me.
You are Majestic, royalty above all royalty.
You are Everywhere, all around, with us in everything we do and
watching out for us every step of the way.
God, you are
AWESOME.

TODAY'S SPECIAL

Time to choose

Luke 3:15-17, 21-22: The baptism of Jesus

Equipment:
postcards
paper plates
shaving foam
large plastic sheet
paper and pen
blindfolds
music and lyrics

Pick about ten cards and randomly write either: north, south, east or west on each card. On another set of cards write a number from 1 to 10. Prepare a number of paper plates by spraying a large mound of shaving foam onto the plates. Spread the large plastic sheet over the floor. Ask for several volunteers from the group. Blindfold each of the volunteers and ask them to remove their shoes and socks. Place the paper plates in a random pattern onto the floor covering.

Position each volunteer at various points around the room. Select another member of the group and ask them to choose a direction card (N S E W) and ask another group member to select a number card. The first volunteer must face the direction indicated by the first card and then walk the number of steps as directed on the second card. Continue this for each volunteer.

You might like to have a bowl of water and a towel available!

(Allow 10 minutes for this activity.)

Changing direction can be a bit difficult (not to mention messy) at times. Have a look at 'All I have in this world' by Martin Smith (*World Wide Worship No. 1*) or 'Turn our hearts' by Graham Kendrick (*The source*, 531).

(Allow approximately 5 minutes.)

Do the lyrics of the songs have anything to say about a change of direction?

Read Luke 3:15-17, 21-22.
John the Baptist was causing a bit of a stir. He was big, loud and didn't mind speaking the truth, even though he knew it would upset people.

Many people thought that he was the Messiah, the expected champion or saviour of the Jews. John would have nothing to do with this idea (see verse 16). So, if that was the case, why did Jesus go to John to be baptised?

Many of the people John baptised chose to be thrown in the river Jordan as a way of saying, 'I'm choosing God's way for my life' and, in much the same way, this is what Jesus did.

At the age of 12 Jesus was found asking questions and listening to the discussions in the temple. After that time he returned to Nazareth and continued with his life as a carpenter. It was eighteen years later that he recognised that God's purpose for him on earth was about to be revealed.

As Jesus was about to be baptised, God spoke to him. God confirmed that what Jesus was about to do was the right choice. First, God made it clear that Jesus was his own son. This was confirmation of who he was and who had sent him. Second, God said that he was really pleased with the choice that Jesus had made. Jesus chose God's way because he knew that it was the only way to go. The first words that God spoke are echoed in Psalm 2:7: 'You are my son, because today I have become your father.' The second statement is found in Isaiah 42:1: 'Here is my servant! I have made him strong. He is my chosen one; I am pleased with him.'

John the Baptist showed the way, Jesus became the way to God and we are given the choice of going God's way.

Have a flipchart available. Ask the group what situations, feelings, concerns, worries or problems can prevent us from choosing to go God's way?

- Is it the fear of not being in control of our own life?
- Is it a worry about what other people will think of us?
- Do we have problems with the whole concept of 'God'?
- Does God feel too distant or too busy to be bothered about us as individuals?
- If God is so real, why do we hurt so much?
- Why do people suffer?

Try and encourage the group to be as honest and open as possible. Write down whatever 'barriers' are suggested as causing the group a problem about choosing God's way.

(Allow 5 minutes.)

There is absolutely nothing wrong with having questions which need answers. Sometimes there aren't responses which answer our questions fully.

Give each member of the group a piece of paper and a pen and ask them to write down one question which makes it difficult for them to relate to God in any way. When they have written the question, ask them to fold the paper and place it in the palm of their hand. Suggest that they might like to think about the question while you read the following prayer:

God,
  a lot of the time,
  I just can't get a handle on you.
I can't find answers to the questions
  that rumble around my head
  making everything appear unclear,
  difficult to see, hard to understand.
If only I could speak to you
  face to face;
  ask some of those questions
  that are burning my tongue;
  see what it is you want me to see;
  put things into perspective
  so that my image of you
  isn't quite so distorted.
I don't want to feel afraid
  that my honesty
  causes you, and other people,
  a problem.
I think that
  if my questions cause them a problem,
  that's not my problem but theirs.
I'm waiting, listening.
Please tell me what you think
  and that way
  at least we're talking
  which, if what I hear is right,
  is what you wanted
  in the first place!

TODAY'S SPECIAL

He did what?

John 2:1-11: Jesus at a wedding in Cana

Equipment:
paper and pens
small cross
music and lyrics

Prepare several sheets of paper by writing one of the sentences below at the top of each sheet.

1. I found a banana skin on the floor and . . .
2. When I woke up this morning, I yawned and . . .
3. I swallowed a marshmallow and . . .
4. I brushed my hair and . . .
5. After I finished reading my book, I rubbed my eyes and . . .
6. I washed my face and . . .
7. I started to squeeze the spot and . . .
8. I felt really sick and I . . .
9. I took the piece of cotton wool and . . .
10. I gargled the water and . . .

Distribute one sheet of paper to each member of the group. Don't let anyone show their neighbour what is written on their own piece of paper. Ask each group member to think of a response to the sentence but *don't* let them write the response on their own piece of paper. Get them to pass their sheet of paper to the person on their left. When they receive their neighbour's paper, they should write the response they thought of for their sentence on that piece of paper!

Have the group read the results aloud. Should be good for a laugh.

(Allow 5 minutes for this activity.)

Sometimes people do such amazing things and we are often left in a state of wonder.

Take a look at 'For all that you've done' by Dennis Jernigan (*The source*, 108) or 'You are mighty' by Craig Musseau (*The source*, 594).

(Allow approximately 5 minutes.)

It's almost impossible to be prepared to expect the unexpected. When people behave in a way which is totally different from what we expect, then we are often left feeling confused, perplexed or even disappointed.

Read John 2:1-11.

The wedding at Cana was one of those occasions which Jesus was expected to attend because the family had been invited. You can imagine the look on his face when Mary told him to go and get himself ready: 'Oh, do I have to go?'

For the two people getting married this was a major celebration. Both during the wedding ceremony and afterwards the couple would be treated like royalty. They would even be dressed in special robes and wear crowns. On such an occasion it was important for everything to go according to plan. Everything had to be done properly. It was really important not to disappoint your guests when the celebrations could last for several days. So it wasn't only the couple who were to be married that looked forward to the occasion.

In a village or town, it was almost certain that you would get an invite to attend the wedding of any family member or friend. It was accepted practice that, if you were invited to their wedding, you were obliged to return their hospitality and provide a similar quality and quantity of food and wine.

The wedding at Cana was really the first public appearance for Jesus and his disciples. The disciples must have wondered what they were doing there. Jesus had recruited them to join with him as he set about his ministry and here they were doing the social domestic bit. Not only that, but rather than show some authority or perform an outstanding miracle that would have the Romans shaking in their boots, Jesus is on the receiving end of his mother's worries about the host's wine supplies. His reaction is to ask his mother not to tell him what to do, especially not in front of the disciples! (Parents never change.)

But, rather than see the hosts embarrassed, Jesus performs a miracle that would have made the authorities laugh rather than suspect that here was the Saviour.

Jesus doesn't ask for the local newspaper to be there or demand that this miracle should be performed in front of large crowds. In fact, the guests are unaware that a miracle has happened, all they know is that the best wine has been brought out last.

Think about it. Jesus dealt with a situation that would have caused a lot of embarrassment and possible financial problems if the hosts had had to send out for more expensive wine. Jesus hasn't changed. He still wants to be with us in situations that we find difficult or in problems that are likely to cause pain.

Provide each member of the group with a piece of paper and a pen. Ask the group to think about a situation or a problem that is giving them some grief at the moment and write it on the paper. Fold the paper. Place a small cross on a table in the centre of the room and ask the group to place their piece of paper at the bottom of the cross.

(Allow 5 minutes.)

Ask the group to be quiet and to think about the problem or situation which they've written on the paper. While they are quiet, read the following:

Psalm 69:13-17.
But I pray to you, Lord.
So when the time is right, answer me
  and help me with your wonderful love.
Don't let me sink in the mud,
  but save me from my enemies
  and from the deep water.
Don't let me be swept away by a flood
  or drowned in the ocean or swallowed by death.

Answer me, Lord! You are kind and good.
Pay attention to me! You are truly merciful.
Don't turn away from me.
I am your servant, and I am in trouble.
Please hurry and help!

TODAY'S SPECIAL

Release!

Luke 4:14-21: Jesus begins his work

Equipment:
flipchart
marker pen
candles
music and lyrics

Divide the group into two teams. Team A must choose six film titles. Team B have to guess what the title is by asking yes-or-no questions. For example: 'Is it a romance?'; 'Does it involve a dog?'. Team B are given five attempts (questions) to guess the film title correctly. If they fail to guess the film, then one of the team must 'go to prison' and sit away from the group and not contribute to their team. If Team B correctly guess the film title then they can 'release' a team member already in prison or, if they haven't got a team member in prison, they can use the correct guess to 'get out of prison free'. You might like the teams to swap over after a few minutes.

(Allow 10 minutes for this activity.)

It can be really frustrating not being able to contribute or help people out of a problem.

Try having a look at 'Jesus Christ' by Matt Redman (*Re:source 2000*, 7) or 'The price is paid' by Graham Kendrick (*The source*, 487).

(Allow approximately 5 minutes.)

Ask those members of the group who found themselves 'in prison' what it felt like to be isolated from the rest of the team.

Read Luke 4:14-21.
News was spreading all over the place about Jesus and what he was doing. He didn't need TV or a newspaper to 'advertise' what he was up to in Galilee – his actions spoke louder and had a greater impact than any words.

On his return to his home in Nazareth, many people must have been pleased to see such a popular figure. The leaders of the synagogue would have felt quite pleased that someone with such a growing reputation was making a visit.

It seemed to be the custom that any adult with anything to say could participate in the service. Jesus read from Isaiah 61:1-2. He appeared to emphasise the words 'me' in verse 1. Imagine Jesus reading this piece of scripture:

'The Lord's Spirit has come to *me*,
because he has chosen *me*
to tell the good news to the poor.
The Lord has sent *me* to announce freedom for prisoners . . .'

Isaiah 61 is known as a Jubilee text. Every 50 years the freeing of slaves was announced, debts were cancelled and land was returned to its original owners.

Jesus is making a statement. He's telling everyone that he has come to restore what has been lost. To put things back where they belong. On one level, Jesus is insisting that those who want to follow him should give back what they have taken dishonestly, and redistribute wealth so that those living in poverty can be 'released' from the economic 'chains' which bind them. But on another level, he is making the point that he wants to bring release to those who are feeling isolated because of emotional hurts and physical problems. Most importantly, he wants to restore a relationship that has been lost, the relationship between ourselves and God the Father.

The statement Jesus made in the synagogue was controversial then and it's controversial now.

Have a flipchart available. Ask the group to think of individuals, groups and cultures which are suffering injustice or persecution. For example: ethnic minorities, the homeless, people working for low wages, the abused, and those people deprived of basic needs, such as healthcare, housing and freedom.

Make a list of all the group's suggestions.

(Allow 5 minutes.)

Have the 'suggestions' displayed in a central place for all the group to see. Ask one member of the group to light a candle for one of their suggestions. As that member of the group lights the candle, ask the rest of the group to say with you:

'May you see God's light shine in your darkness.'

Continue so that each group member has lit a candle and each of the suggestions has been prayed for.

TODAY'S SPECIAL

Out of the ordinary

Luke 2:22-40: Simeon praises the Lord

Equipment:
selection of toilet rolls
squares of newspaper
music and lyrics

Ask for three or four volunteers from the group. Explain to the volunteers that they are about to take part in a consumer test which may have an amazing impact on the development of future products.

Blindfold the volunteers and sit them to one side of the room. Lay out a selection of toilet rolls on a table. The selection should contain samples from as many different brands as possible. Try to have a range of samples which varies from total luxury to sheets of cut-up newspaper.

Ask one blindfolded volunteer at a time to feel the paper and then try and identify which is the luxury paper and which is the newspaper. Repeat with the other volunteers.

When you have completed the 'test' ask the volunteers to take off their blindfolds and now repeat the test. Was it easier to identify the different papers without the blindfold? Or was it just the same with and without the blindfold?

(Allow 10 minutes for this activity.)

Most of the volunteers should have been able to identify the newspaper from the luxury paper even with the blindfold. We rely on our senses to help us appreciate and understand the world around us. But, sometimes, we may need a little more than just our senses to help us.

Have a look at 'Men of faith' by Martin Smith (*The source,* 354) or 'I walk by faith' by Chris Falson (*The source*, 253).

(Allow approximately 5 minutes for this.)

Ask the group how they could tell the difference between the different rolls of toilet paper.

Read Luke 2:22-40.
After the birth of a baby, Jewish tradition dictated that the mother of the child was to stay at home and not take part in any religious festivals for 40 days, if the child was a boy, or 80 days if the child was a girl. After that time the mother took part in a ceremony called 'purification after childbirth'. The mother had to go to the temple and give a lamb as a burnt offering and a young pigeon for a sin offering. The offering of a lamb was quite an expense and not everyone would have been able to afford it, so an alternative was to offer two pigeons. This was known as 'the offering of the poor'. Verse 24 of the reading states that this is precisely what Mary and Joseph did. This indicates that Jesus didn't come from a wealthy home or have all the trimmings which would have made him appear anything other than another baby from an ordinary family.

Simeon was an old man who believed that God would one day send someone who would become the 'champion' of Israel. This 'champion' would be 'Christ the Lord' (Christ meaning 'chosen' or 'anointed' and Lord meaning 'having power and authority'). So, Simeon knew that God intended to send a very special person, someone chosen by God and having God's authority to carry out God's instructions.

With these indications to go on you could easily get an idea of someone who stood out from the crowd, someone who looked and sounded different from the rest. God's Spirit tells Simeon to go to the temple and meet this 'special' person. Various images must have been going through Simeon's head as he approached the temple. Simeon was a man who studied the Bible (Old Testament) and spent time praying. He would have been aware of the prophet Micah and his writings, which said the Lord would choose someone from Bethlehem to become the 'Shepherd of Israel' who would care for his people' (see Micah 5:2-5).

When Simeon got to the temple he would have been looking for a young child, but in a city the size of Jerusalem there must have been a lot of parents bringing their children to the temple. How would Simeon know where to look? How would Simeon recognise this special child? Would he have expected the child to belong to a poor family?

We're not told how Simeon eventually recognised the child Jesus. But we are told that Simeon was delighted and praised God when he took hold of the child in his arms.

Jesus lived an ordinary life in most ways and experienced the difficulties that most people felt. He was fully aware of how hard life could be and how insecure people could feel when there didn't seem to be enough money or work to provide for the family's needs. Whatever the problems or difficulties, Jesus knew about them and experienced them – and today he wants to be with us no matter what our circumstances.

FOURTH SUNDAY OF EPIPHANY

Write the word 'faith' on a piece of paper and display it on the wall. Ask the group what they think the word means and, most importantly, what role does it have in their life?

Encourage the group to be honest even if that means some of the group saying that faith doesn't mean anything at all to them.

(Allow 5 minutes.)

Suggest to the group that they might like to spend a few moments thinking about faith and what it means to them as individuals. After a short while read the following prayer:

Lord,
   can I trust you?
You know, when things get hard,
   out of hand
   and just a bit messy?
Can I trust you
   when my head thumps
   from the millions of hassles
   that cloud my day?
Can I trust you
   when my eyes are tired and my brain aches
   and my feet want to give up and go home?
Can I trust you
   when I feel cold, lonely,
   unlovely, hurt and scared?
Can I trust you
   when everything I try to do
   and everything I try to say
   just make things worse?
Lord, can I trust you
   to keep me safe,
   to protect me from harm,
   to sort out the hassle and the grief?
Lord, be with me.

TODAY'S SPECIAL

Don't do that, do this!

Luke 5:1-11: Jesus chooses his first disciples

Equipment:
cards
flipchart
music and lyrics or drama sketch

Write an instruction on each of the cards. Some ideas are listed below:

1. Stick your fingers in your ears and recite a nursery rhyme.
2. Touch your left foot with your right hand and your right foot with your left hand.
3. Stand on a chair and flap your arms up and down.
4. Try and touch your nose with your tongue.
5. Suck a sweet and hold your nose at the same time.
6. Walk around the room holding your ankles.
7. Sit on a chair and pretend to shiver. Wrap your arms around you and keep saying, 'It's so cold in here'.
8. Keep telling everyone that it's far too hot in the room. Ask to have the door and windows open.
9. Hold your head in your hands and tell everyone that there's going to be an explosion.
10. Form circles with your fingers, place them in front of your eyes, like binoculars, and ask everyone if they've seen the No. 45 bus.

Distribute the cards to the group and ask them to obey/perform the instructions on the cards all at the same time.

Ask the group members how they felt about the instructions. Did any of the group refuse to take part? Why?

(Allow 10 minutes for this activity.)

Sometimes being given an instruction is neither easy nor fun. Often we feel annoyed at being asked to do something we don't want to do or don't know why we're being asked to do it.

Take a look at 'Here I am' by Chris Bowater (*The source*, 161) or 'I will seek you' by Matthew Lockwood (*The source*, 267). Alternatively, you might like to use the drama sketch *The Wrinklies at the seaside* (see page 49).

If someone offers you advice you can thank them and then get on with doing things as you were. If someone simply tells you that you're not doing something right and that you should do it another way . . . that can irritate.

Read Luke 5:1-11.
Lake Gennesaret (another name for Lake Galilee) is often described as a beautiful place. It's located next to a very fertile area which the Jews sometimes called 'the prince of gardens' and its waves were described as 'the voice of a harp'. In other words, quite a nice place to take a stroll or have a picnic.

Jesus was becoming well known for the wisdom of his words and for his controversial actions (see Luke 4:31-44). He was a person whom other people would travel quite a distance just to see and hear. There would already have been quite a few people around the lake as Jesus arrived. Apart from the casual visitors, there were many people whose livelihood depended on the lake. Into this mixture of leisure and work walked Jesus. He gathered crowds around him almost immediately. Some of the fishermen had been fishing all night and they were busily cleaning their nets ready for the next night, looking forward to getting some sleep. The crowd became so large that Jesus had to persuade the fishermen to take a boat and row him a short distance from the shore. Simon wasn't too happy. He told Jesus he'd been up all night and hadn't even caught a cold. Jesus told the experienced fisherman to let the nets down over the side of the boat. Can you imagine what Simon must have thought: 'What do you think I've been doing all night?' Rather than argue, Simon dropped the nets over the side and suddenly there were more fish than net. He called for help and soon two boats were so full of fish they began to sink. Simon and his mates were stunned. You would have thought that Simon would have offered Jesus a job there and then. But, recognising that something special had happened, Simon knelt before Jesus and called him 'Lord'.

And then, having just caught the largest catch of fish they had ever seen, Jesus asked Simon and his mates to pull up their boats, put their nets away and follow him!

What some people thought was going to be just another day at the lake, and others thought was just another wasted night, turned out to be 24 hours they'd never forget.

Ask the group how they would have felt if they'd been Simon.

- Would they have given up their jobs and followed Jesus?
- Would they have turned their back on their friends and family and walked wherever Jesus wanted to go?
- Why did Simon and some of his mates decide to follow Jesus?
- Do you think the crowd had a huge barbecue that night with all that fish?
- Why is it difficult to do something just because someone asks you to?
- What pressures are there which make it hard to follow Jesus?

(Allow 5 minutes.)

You might like to put some of the group's responses onto a flipchart. While the group consider some of their thoughts and ideas, read the following extract from Proverbs:

Proverbs 4:10-15.
My child, if you listen and obey my teachings,
  you will live a long time.
I have shown you the way that makes sense;
  I have guided you along the right path.
Your road won't be blocked,
  and you won't stumble when you run.
Hold firmly to my teaching and never let go.
It will mean life for you.
Don't follow the bad example of cruel and evil people.
Turn aside and keep going. Stay away from them.

THE WRINKLIES AT THE SEASIDE

Characters Two aged grumps who are feeling slightly less grumpy than normal, until things start to happen which alter that!

Scene The two Wrinklies are at the seaside. They are sitting by the edge of the water, dangling their feet and basking in the sun; they have the proverbial knotted hankie on their heads and have rolled up their trousers. A small picnic is laid out next to them.

Props
tablecloth for the picnic
selection of picnic-type food
glasses of fruit juice
knotted hankies
baggy trousers
braces
holey vest

Old 1 This is the life.

Old 2 *(Leans back and sighs)* You're telling me.

Old 1 I know I am, you daft gerbil.

Old 2 Know what?

Old 1 I'm telling you.

Old 2 Telling me what?

Old 1 Is this going to go on all day?

Old 2 What?

Old 1 I take it back.

Old 2 *(Scratches head)* What?

Old 1	I didn't mean it.
Old 2	*(Scratches chin)* Mean what?
Old 1	To insult gerbils.
Old 2	You've been in the sun too long, mate.
Old 1	At least I've got an excuse.
Old 2	*(Looks up at the sun and squints)* Nice weather.
Old 1	You're telling me!
Old 2	*(Paddles feet)* Nice day for it.
Old 1	Couldn't be better.
Old 2	Well, it could.
Old 1	*(Looks around and points)* You mean all these people?
Old 2	Yeah, spoils the view.
Old 1	Just when you want a bit of peace and quiet.
Old 2	Only to be expected really.
Old 1	What is?
Old 2	All these people.
Old 1	*(Grimace)* Typical, bit of sun and they think they have a right to invade our privacy.
Old 2	Could be worse.
Old 1	How's that then?
Old 2	They could have brought their donkeys.

Old 1 Ought to be a law against it.

Old 2 You'd think they'd at least bring a shovel with them.

Old 1 I ain't having them build daft sandcastles all over the place. Nuisance they are.

Old 2 I meant the donkeys.

Old 1 *(Look of surprise on face)* They build sandcastles?

Old 2 No, you hairless hamster, I mean to clear up after them.

Old 1 What, like that one over there. *(Points to one side)*

Old 2 *(Waves hand in the direction Old 1 is pointing)* Oi, clear off and drop that somewhere else.

Old 1 *(Holds nose)* Trust the wind to be in the wrong direction.

Old 2 *(Points to the other side)* Hey-up, it's that bloke they've all been talking about.

Old 1 Just our luck, now we'll never get any peace.

Old 2 It might be worth having a listen. I hear he's quite a good talker.

Old 1 It ain't talk we need, it's action.

Old 2 Too hot for that.

Old 1 Maybe, but words are nothing more than hot air unless you're prepared to put 'em into action.

Old 2 I reckon that's what he's trying to say.

Old 1 What's he saying then?

Old 2 *(Cups hand to ear)* Something about loving those who get you angry and all worked up.

Old 1 He obviously doesn't know anyone with a donkey then. *(Waves hand in front of nose)*

Old 2 Well, there's plenty of people listening to him.

Old 1 There would be.

Old 2 Why's that?

Old 1 Bit of entertainment.

Old 2 I don't reckon he's that entertaining. Hard words for some folk.

Old 1 That's as maybe, but you don't get anywhere in this world by rattling too many cages.

Old 2 Nah, doesn't do to upset folk. *(Raises voice)* Not like some people here who think this beach is public property.

Old 1 It is.

Old 2 *(Waves hands as if to push people away)* Get out of it. Be careful, *(starts to scratch)* I've got something catching. Terrible it is.

TODAY'S SPECIAL

That's a tall order!

Luke 6:17-26: Blessings and troubles

Equipment:
bag of marshmallows
cards
stones
small cross
music and lyrics

Prepare a series of questions and write them on the cards. Ask the group to divide into pairs. Nominate one of the pair to ask questions and the other to answer.

Sample questions (only require a 'yes' or 'no' answer):

1. Most lipstick contains fish scales. (yes)
2. Bats always turn left when leaving a cave. (yes)
3. Taphephobia is the fear of taps. (no, fear of being buried alive)
4. Pinocchio is the Italian for 'pine eye'. (yes)
5. The longest recorded flight of a chicken is two minutes. (no, 13 seconds)
6. Slugs have four noses. (yes)
7. A jellyfish is made out of silicon. (no, 95 per cent water)
8. In Tokyo, they sell toupees for dogs. (yes)
9. Fingernails grow nearly ten times faster than toenails. (no, four times faster)
10. Dolphins sleep with both eyes open. (no, just one eye open)

The person answering the question nods their head for a yes answer and shakes their head for a no. If they answer correctly they are given a marshmallow, BUT . . . they cannot eat it. The questioner places the marshmallow on their partner's tongue. The partner must keep their tongue sticking out until they have answered another question correctly, then they can eat the marshmallow. If they answer a question incorrectly, they have another marshmallow placed on top of the first. The questioner must not help their partner in any way! You might like to have the partners reverse roles after a few questions.

(Allow 10 minutes for this activity.)

We can be asked to do strange and difficult things at times!

Have a look at 'Let your love come down' by Noel and Tricia Richards (*The source*, 319) or 'This is the message of the cross' by Martin Smith (*The source*, 518).

(Allow approximately 5 minutes for this.)

Jesus was keen to point out the fact that following him wasn't going to be the easiest thing to do.

Read Luke 6:17-26.

Jesus was becoming a major attraction. His reputation had spread beyond Galilee to the coast and to the south of the country. Large crowds gathered to hear and see what Jesus could do for them.

Jesus didn't want to be well known or popular simply because he could sort out people's problems. He wanted the people to understand what he was about. He started by discussing ways in which God would 'bless' the people. It was quite a common tradition to use the word 'bless' to indicate something that was pleasing to God. Jesus was concerned that people should have a right relationship with God, and not one which simply consisted of everybody waiting to see what God could do for them. Jesus wanted to change the way people viewed their relationship with God. He started by saying that God would bless those people who weren't smug and complacent about their life. He particularly pointed at those people who thought that they had a special place in God's affections because they were wealthy and had plenty to eat. It was sometimes thought that wealth was an indication that God was pleased with you and not that you'd possibly conned your wealth out of the poor!

Jesus then goes on to state that following him and having a relationship with God will often mean being misunderstood and finding the going tough. Following God was never intended to be based on a rule book but an attitude of heart. It starts with the recognition that without God we have nothing of real value and that our lifestyle must reflect God's love. That's a tall order.

Write the word 'wealth' on a flipchart. Ask the group to define what 'wealth' means.

- How can wealth affect the way we behave?
- Can it affect the way we act towards other people?
- Does it mean that we feel somehow different from other people?
- Can wealth be a barrier which separates us from other people?

Write some of the group's thoughts on the flipchart.

(Allow 5 minutes.)

Give each group member a stone. Ask the group to think about some of the problems or issues that create a barrier between ourselves and God. The stone represents those problems which weigh us down and cause us to feel fed-up and the personal issues which blind us to the needs of others.

Ask the group to listen to the following prayer and, if they feel able, to place their stone at the base of the cross as a prayer that God would help them see things from his point of view.

OK, Lord
    so what's going on?
Why do I feel this way?
It can't be all my fault, can it?
Well, see it my way:
    if I spend all my time
    wondering what other people think or feel,
    how will I ever get
    to where I want to go?
How will I ever get what I want?
Although I have to admit
    that at times I feel like I'm chewing sand,
    or walking through treacle.
Perhaps I shouldn't struggle
    and keep yelling in your ear.
Perhaps I should listen,
    take the time to see and hear
    just how much you love me,
    and him and her.

TODAY'S SPECIAL

That's the way to do it!

Luke 6:27-38: Love for enemies

Equipment:
cards
pens and paper
envelopes
notice board and pins
music and lyrics

Prepare the cards by writing one of the following words on each one:

straight	tall	ugly	hard	narrow
small	wide	deep	wet	dry
shallow	beautiful	twisted	dark	
light	open	shut	soft	

Divide the group into two teams. Shuffle the cards. One team member from Group A selects a card and mimes the word on the card to their group. The rest of Group A try to guess the mime but, to win a point, they must answer with the opposite of the mimed word! If they answer with the mimed word they lose a point. If they cannot guess, the other group are allowed to guess. The teams take it in turns to guess the opposite of the mimed word and score or lose points accordingly.

(Allow 10 minutes for this activity.)

Trying to do the opposite of what you expect is never easy. Have a look at 'A new commandment' (*The source*, 23) or 'We want to remain in your love' by Andy Piercy and Dave Clifton (*The source*, 558).

(Allow approximately 5 minutes for this.)

You might like to start this section with a quick game of 'Simon Says' but the group must act the mirror image of what you do, e.g. if you rub your head in a clockwise motion, they must do it anti-clockwise or if you touch your nose with your left hand, they must use their right.

Read Luke 6:27-38.
Jesus continues talking to the disciples and all the people gathered around Lake Galilee. He's already given them plenty to think about when he drops another thought into their heads: 'Love your enemies'!

He starts by saying: 'If you really want to hear what I've got to say, then grab a load of this. Don't do what you've always been told to do; do what I tell you, which is the right way to live. Be good to everyone who hates you!'

Can you just imagine what the crowd were thinking? Some probably suggested that Jesus had been in the sun too long! Most of the people in the crowd would have been familiar with the teaching of the Pharisees (a group of ordinary people whose strict interpretation of the law, based on the *Torah* or first five books of the Old Testament, led to an obsession with rules concerning every detail of life) and an influential religious group called the *Essenes* (they believed that God was about to come and establish his kingdom on earth and only the really pure and most worthy Jews would be part of it). These two groups had a very 'them and us' attitude. They looked down on anyone who didn't meet their high standards and ideals. Jesus emphasised that it was important to treat other people the way God does and not expect them to keep a bucket-load of rules before you'd even say 'hello' to them.

Just because some people don't act or behave the way we like them to doesn't mean that God cares for them any less than he cares for us. It's far from easy being considerate to those people who really get up our nose, but Jesus is asking us to make a difference; not to react how other people expect us to, but to react as God would expect us to. See the difference?

Give each member of the group a pen, paper and envelope. Ask them to make a list of all the people they find difficult to accept as friends, family, human beings! Place the paper in the envelope and stick/pin the envelopes onto a notice board. Without asking the group to identify who's on their list, ask them what it is about these people that they find so difficult. Be sensitive to certain issues that may involve family or even other members of the group.

(Allow 5 minutes.)

When you've finished discussing the issues raised, suggest that the group think about how God would react to those people and situations. Is it possible to see those people from God's point of view? Ask the group to reflect on God's behaviour to us and others while you read the following prayer:

Lord, it's difficult enough
trying to cope with myself
without having to understand,
appreciate, care and become friends
with all those people who really
get up my nose, irritate and generally
make me feel as if I've eaten
a few too many jam doughnuts.

Your idea of that funny word,
you know, that *thingy* word,
the one you talk about so much
(I don't want to say the word,
because if I do
you just might make me behave
like I know the word
and want to act
like that *thingy* word).

Why should I go out of my way
to be *thingy*
to everyone whom you *thingy*?
Thingy makes me feel funny
as if I've done something
odd, different, not normal,
something out of the ordinary
and definitely not the way to behave
if you want street-cred
with all those other people
who don't use that *thingy* word.

But just suppose,
not for real you understand,
just pretend that I knew what *thingy*
really meant,
I suppose it might, just might
make a difference.

TODAY'S SPECIAL

Going down a storm!

Luke 8:22-25: A storm

Equipment:
flipchart
table-tennis balls
bowl of water
music and lyrics or drama sketch

Write a list of phobias from the selection below. Don't write the meaning of the phobia, that's for the group to try and guess.

Monophobia	(fear of loneliness)
Nyctophobia	(fear of darkness)
Zelophobia	(fear of jealousy)
Ergophobia	(fear of work)
Algophobia	(fear of pain)
Scopophobia	(fear of being looked at)
Ochlophobia	(fear of crowds)
Thanatophobia	(fear of death)
Kakorraphiaphobia	(fear of failure)
Odontophobia	(fear of teeth)

The group might have a lot of fun just trying to pronounce some of these words!

Reveal one phobia name at a time and see if the group can guess what the phobia is a fear of. You might like to have a go at inventing some of your own phobias, e.g. footaphobia (fear of football), brussophobia (fear of brussels sprouts) or even soapophobia (fear of soap operas).

(Allow 10 minutes for this activity.)

Being afraid shouldn't be something to fear! It's how we deal with fear that is important. Take a look at 'Hold me closer to you' by Noel and Tricia Richards (*The source*, 172) or 'You are my rock' by Jarrod Cooper and Sharon Pearce (*The source*, 597). You might also like to have a look at the drama sketch *The Wrinklies go sailing* (see page 62).

(Allow approximately 5 minutes for this.)

Have a brief chat with the group about fear. What is fear? Why do we get afraid? What kind of things make us afraid?

Read Luke 8:22-25.
It seemed like a good idea at the time. What could be better than sailing on the lake and having a bit of relaxation?

Jesus had suggested sailing across to the other side of Lake Galilee to an area populated by non-Jews. With him, amongst the disciples, were Peter, James and John, experienced sailors who knew the lake well. It was only natural that Jesus felt confident in the ability of the three disciples and allowed himself to catch up on some much needed rest.

Without warning, a storm appeared and threatened to sink the boat. This couldn't have been a run-of-the-mill storm. Peter and the others would have experienced many storms and lived to tell the tale. This storm must have been something out of the ordinary to frighten the sailors. Even with all their knowledge and skills they became so afraid that they turned to the only person they thought could help.

They didn't turn to Jesus because he was an amazing sailor or had any astounding skills when it came to weather forecasting. The disciples turned to Jesus because they had seen him perform miracles which defied logic.

The Bible verses simply tell us that Jesus got up and ordered the storm to stop making a nuisance of itself. From storm to calm within seconds and, having had his sleep ruined, Jesus merely asked the disciples why they didn't have any faith! They'd seen what he could do before, why couldn't they trust him to deal with this situation? Perhaps the disciples thought that if he was asleep he wasn't aware of the danger they were all in? Possibly, because all the other miracles had occurred on dry land, they didn't know if he understood the true threat of the lake?

Jesus calmed the storm and reassured the disciples that they were safe in his hands. A lesson for us all?

If we take the word 'storm' to mean any situation that causes unrest, discomfort or holds a threat, can the group think of 'storms' in their lives that are giving them cause for concern?

Do any of the group want to talk about the situation? Have any other members of the group experienced something similar? If so, how did they deal with it?

If it's appropriate, give each member of the group one of the table-tennis balls and a marker pen. Suggest that they write their name on the ball and place it in the bowl of water.

(Allow 5 minutes.)

While the group think about the 'storm(s)' which affect their lives, read the following prayer:

Lord,
I realise it sounds daft,
possibly really stupid
in the warm light of the day,
but I just can't help
looking behind me
whenever I walk upstairs to bed.
Now, please don't laugh,
I know it's irrational,
that there's nothing there,
but you never know,
one day there just might be
something which will throw my life
into confusion, disarray,
and make it seem like
the sun's gone to sleep.

You see,
the stairs
are my life.
It's my journey
from birth to the future.
And I really need to know
that you're there,
right behind me,
beside me, in front of me,
watching my feet
so that I don't trip over my own shadow.

THE WRINKLIES GO SAILING

Characters	The Wrinklies, who aren't having a good day. It's cold, there are too many people about and getting wet isn't high on their list of pleasurable experiences.
Scene	The two aged grumps are standing at the edge of Lake Galilee. Both are dressed in waterproof gear: wellingtons, raincoat, hat and gloves.
Props	waterproof gear oar or paddle thermos flask sign saying *Lake Galilee*

Old 1 Are you sure about this? *(Nods head to indicate lake in front of him)*

Old 2 What's up, got cold feet?

Old 1 It's wet feet I'm bothered about.

Old 2 I keep telling you, there's absolutely nothing to worry about.

Old 1 That's why I'm worried.

Old 2 What?

Old 1 You, you keep saying it's going to be OK.

Old 2 Well it is. All I'm doing is reassuring you, giving you a bit of confidence.

Old 1 That's a laugh to start with.

Old 2 What?

Old 1 You giving anyone confidence.

Old 2	Cheek! I was learning to sail when half of these young fishermen were still in their cots being fed camel's milk and mashed fig.
Old 1	Nothing much changed there then.
Old 2	*(Licks finger and holds it above head)* Plenty of wind.
Old 1	*(Puzzled frown)* Eh?
Old 2	*(Stern look)* North-easterly breeze.
Old 1	Thank goodness for that.
Old 2	Told you, I know what I'm doing.
Old 1	*(Nods to left)* More than I can say for that lot.
Old 2	*(Looks in same direction)* Young 'uns today. Give 'em a couple of barrels and a plank of wood and they reckon they're ready to sail the oceans.
Old 1	Looks like that lot are branching out into the ferry business.
Old 2	What makes you say that?
Old 1	Look! *(Points with oar)* They're taking passengers.
Old 2	Hey up, it's that teacher fella. You know, the one everybody's talking about.
Old 1	Perhaps he's taking a holiday, getting away from it all.
Old 2	Just look at 'em.
Old 1	It's like a circus on water.
Old 2	Well, I just hope they haven't brought the elephants with them.

Old 1	*(Points with oar)* I think they already have. Just look at the size of that bloke.
Old 2	Looks like he eats whatever they catch.
Old 1	*(Shivers)* He's more likely to catch a cold today. I reckon there's a storm brewing.
Old 2	*(Looks at sky)* Are you sure?
Old 1	Course I'm sure. Me knees are playing up again. Definitely a sign of bad weather.
Old 2	You can't trust them knees of yours. The last time they played up you walked around in your waterproof gear in the middle of a heatwave.
Old 1	My knees are more reliable than your big toe.
Old 2	Just a moment. My big toe has never been known to be wrong.
Old 1	Tell that to your socks.
Old 2	Who was it that forecast that thunderstorm last month? And who was it that warned you of gales last winter?
Old 1	It was her down the market. There's always going to be bad weather when her eyes meet in the middle. *(Goes cross-eyed)*
Old 2	In that case we must be in for a prolonged spell of snow. I've never known her eyes look any different.
Old 1	There's a storm coming. Don't say I didn't warn you.
Old 2	You'd better warn that lot over there then. *(Points to left)*
Old 1	They won't listen to the likes of me and you.

Old 2 Well, if there's a storm coming, you won't catch me out on the water.

Old 1 You scared then?

Old 2 Me? Pah! I laugh in the face of danger, I sneer at the thunder-clouds.

Old 1 And you get soaked as well.

Old 2 That too.

Old 1 Anyway, you're scared to get out of bed some mornings.

Old 2 That's not being scared, that's being prudent.

Old 1 Prudent?

Old 2 There's no point in taking unnecessary risks at my age.

Old 1 *(Again, points to left)* It seems they're determined to take a risk with the weather.

Old 2 If that storm hits them, they'll know about it.

Old 1 They'll need a bit more than a couple of oars to help.

Old 2 Perhaps that teacher fella has got something up his sleeve.

Old 1 If he has, it'd better be a big umbrella.

Old 2 *(Takes thermos flask)* No point in getting wet. Fancy a drink?

TODAY'S SPECIAL

Doh!

Luke 9:28-36, 37-43: The true glory of Jesus

Equipment:
postcards
pens and paper
large envelope
music and lyrics

Write each of the following phrases on a separate card:

1. I feel like a . . .
2. My mouth feels like a . . .
3. After eating, my stomach feels like a . . .
4. Every time I watch TV my head feels like a . . .
5. After I brush my teeth, they feel like a . . .
6. When I sneeze, my nose feels like a . . .

Now, on some of the other cards write:

1. hole in the road.
2. packet of cornflakes.
3. bottle of disinfectant.
4. bag of sawdust.
5. compost bin.
6. bucket of cold custard.

Shuffle the first set of cards and ask a member of the group to select one of the cards. To complete the sentence ask another group member to select a card from the second set of cards (make sure that these cards are face down). Now, read the complete sentence. Replace the used card from the second set of cards and shuffle. Repeat the selection process with other group members. The whole game should raise a laugh or three. You might like to write some of your own sentences and make the second set of cards as wacky as you can.

(Allow 10 minutes for this activity.)

Sometimes it's easier to express our feelings by actions. Some people have attempted to explain how they feel by putting words and music together in a way that reflects an emotion far better than words alone.

Take a look at 'You make my heart feel glad' by Patricia Morgan and Sue Rinaldi (*The source*, 603) or 'I need you more' by Lindell Cooley and Bruce Haynes (*The source*, 226).

(Allow approximately 5 minutes for this.)

Trying to express our emotions, especially to our family and friends, can leave us feeling angry, frustrated or vulnerable.

Read Luke 9:28-43.

Jesus had been really busy. He'd spoken to literally thousands of people, healed the sick and dealt with a whole host of dodgy evil spirits and was now in need of recharging his batteries. Taking Peter, John and James with him, Jesus took a stroll up a mountain to spend some time talking with his heavenly Father.

As with many of us, as soon as their eyelids obeyed gravity, the three disciples were in the land of slumber. While they were creating a few snores, the disciples were unaware that something remarkable was happening to Jesus. Moses and Elijah had appeared and were talking to Jesus about all that was going to happen to him. Peter, James and John suddenly opened their eyes and were confronted by an amazing scene. The disciples must have looked at each other to check whether they were sharing the same dream! Immediately Peter began to talk about making the place special by building three shelters, or tents, to mark the place where something incredible happened. You can imagine what Jesus thought.

Before Peter could get on to the idea of building a hotel, shopping mall (selling replica models of Moses and Elijah) and amusement arcade, God's voice sounded from heaven, telling the three disciples to listen to what Jesus had to say. The three disciples were left speechless (perhaps a good thing, considering what Peter had been talking about).

The next day, Jesus and the disciples came down from the mountain and walked straight into a load of hassle. First, there was a large crowd waiting for Jesus to say something clever; second, a father worried about the demon attacking his son and third, complaints that some of the disciples had tried to deal with the demon but had failed miserably. Again, can you imagine how Jesus felt? Doh! Look at verse 41, as Jesus, in frustration, says to his disciples: 'Why do I have to put up with you?' Bit harsh perhaps, or is Jesus really annoyed that his disciples hadn't been listening to a word he'd said over the past few weeks?

Jesus dealt with the demon, and the boy and his father were amazed at God's authority and power. The interesting thing is that Jesus wasn't above feeling frustrated, annoyed or vulnerable. He wanted to trust his disciples but they were clearly found lacking in the listening and understanding stakes.

Jesus knows how we feel because he's been there already. Quite reassuring really.

Distribute pens and small pieces of paper to each member of the group. Ask the group to think about those areas of their lives where they may feel frustrated, annoyed, vulnerable, confused or hurt. Suggest that they write a single word which sums up the way they feel, e.g. ANGRY.

Ask them to place their piece of paper into a large envelope upon which you have written: 'For the attention of Jesus'. Place the envelope where the whole group can see it.

(Allow 5 minutes.)

Ask the group to be quiet and think about the situation that is causing/has caused them to feel the way they do. Read the following prayer:

OK, Lord,
enough is enough.
I don't like feeling,
thinking, sensing, listening,
the way I do
to all those situations
which drive me up the wall,
through the ceiling and leave my head spinning.
You know how I feel.
You've been there, done that, read the book
and starred in the film.
Please be with me, help me, stand by me.

TODAY'S SPECIAL

If!

Luke 4:1-13: Jesus and the devil

Equipment:
paper and pens
candle
music and lyrics

Give each member of the group a piece of paper and a pen, and ask them to write three statements about their hopes or desires on the piece of paper (don't write any name or initials which might identify the writer). For example:

1. I want to build a boat.
2. I want to become an actor/actress.
3. I want to travel around the world.

When each group member has finished, collect the statements, shuffle them and then distribute them around the group. Ask one group member to read the three statements and see if the rest of the group can guess who wrote the statements. To add a little bit of mystery, have some statements already prepared which are not specific to anyone in the group. These statements could be based on someone you, or the group, knows or be entirely fictitious. Some of these statements could be totally bizarre!

(Allow 10 minutes for this activity.)

How well do we know each other? How well do we know ourselves, particularly when we are faced with a really difficult situation?

Take a look at 'He is the Lord' by Kevin Prosch (*The source,* 159), or 'Is it true today? by Martin Smith (*The source*, 241).

(Allow approximately 5 minutes for this.)

It isn't always easy to be confident or certain about what we know or believe. It's especially difficult to be positive and self-assured when we are in an awkward situation.

Read Luke 4:1-13.

Jesus had just been baptised in the River Jordan and a voice from heaven had said: 'You are my own dear Son, and I am pleased with you' (Luke 3:22), when he goes off into the desert for a few days. This was to be a period of preparation for Jesus and he was possibly looking forward to some time on his own before things started to heat up. No sooner had he put a foot in the sand when the devil starts to have a go at him. Possibly Jesus sighed and thought: 'Well, there goes my peace and quiet!' Having just been acknowledged as God's Son and told that his Father was pleased with him, along comes someone to question everything.

The devil started by saying 'If . . .'. It's a question, a seed of doubt, a prod at Jesus' self-assurance. By then Jesus was hot, tired, hungry and thirsty. It certainly wasn't the best time to start fielding difficult questions. Jesus could quite easily have replied, 'Right now isn't a good time to answer questions' or 'Let me sleep on it', but he knew that he'd have to face these challenges sooner or later. His answers were part reply and part reassurance to himself. He needed to respond to the devil with words that not only refuted the devil's 'if', but also reaffirmed what Jesus knew to be true.

It's important to remember that the words Jesus used in his replies were not just some simple quotes that he recalled from his childhood, but were true statements, an underlining of his knowledge of who he was and what he had to do.

It's never very easy to feel confident when we are in a difficult situation and someone asks awkward questions. You know that when a question starts with either: 'I thought that . . .' or 'Are you sure that . . .' it's going to be tough finding the appropriate answer. There are many situations where it's tough for us to feel confident in what we believe and 'if' we are doing the right thing. Ask the group if they can think of any situations which have made them question what they believe or doubt that they are doing the 'right' thing.

Make a list of some of the following statements and see if any relate to the situations discussed:

- I am God's child. (John 1:12)
- I am Christ's friend. (John 15:15)
- I have been bought with a price. I belong to God. (1 Corinthians 6:19-20)
- I am complete in Christ. (Colossians 2:10)
- I have been forgiven. (Colossians 1:14)
- I am born of God and the evil one cannot touch me. (1 John 5:1, 18)

- I have direct access to God through the Holy Spirit. (Ephesians 2:18)
- I have not been given a spirit of fear, but of power, love and a sound mind. (2 Timothy 1:7)
- I may approach God with boldness and confidence. (Ephesians 3:12)
- I am confident that the good work that God has begun in me will be perfected. (Philippians 1:6)
- I cannot be separated from the love of God. (Romans 8:39)

There are many more Bible verses which you might add to the list.

(Allow 5 minutes.)

Ask the group to reflect on the Bible verses that you have discussed. Light a candle and while the group are quiet, read the following:

Psalm 138:7-8.
I am surrounded by trouble,
 but you protect me against my angry enemies.
With your powerful arm you keep me safe.
You, Lord, will always treat me with kindness.
Your love never fails.
You have made us what we are.
Don't give up on us now!

TODAY'S SPECIAL

A man's gotta do . . .

Luke 13:31-35: Jesus and Herod

Equipment:
clip-on clothes pegs
flipchart
pair of scissors
sticky tape
music and lyrics

Divide the group into three categories: Grabbers, Givers and Goodies. Distribute the clip-on clothes pegs so that every group member has the same number of pegs and ask everyone to put the pegs anywhere on their clothes as long as they are visible (the more pegs each member has the better).

At a given signal, the three groups go around and behave as their name implies. The 'Grabbers' try and take as many pegs as they can and put them onto their clothing, the 'Givers' simply offer their pegs to anyone and the 'Goodies' try and take the pegs that the 'Grabbers' have taken and give them back to the original owner!

It might be advisable to suggest that you are not liable for any torn clothing!

(Allow 10 minutes for this activity.)

Sometimes, feelings of anger, frustration or confusion can distract us from our intended aim or destination. It can be difficult to keep going when everything seems to be against you.

Try having a look at 'Called to a battle' by Noel and Tricia Richards (*The source*, 61) or 'We shall stand' by Graham Kendrick (*The source*, 556). Alternatively, you might like to use the drama sketch *The Wrinklies get upset* (see page 75).

(Allow approximately 5 minutes for this.)

How would we react if what we were doing provoked a threat on our lives? Would we decide that it might be better to live a while longer and take a rain-check on our actions or would we shrug our shoulders and get on with what we intended to do?

Read Luke 13:31-35.
Jesus and the Pharisees had not seen eye to eye during the past few months. Some of them had bad-mouthed Jesus and he'd had a few choice words to say about them and their 'religious' behaviour.

The Jews themselves had defined seven behavioural categories of Pharisee. They called one category the 'Shoulder' Pharisees, because whatever good deed or act of kindness that they did, they made sure everyone knew about it. There were the 'Hang on a minute' Pharisees who played the game of 'put it off' whenever it came to helping someone or parting with money. Another category were the 'Bruised' Pharisees who thought that looking at a woman was sinful and so closed their eyes whenever they saw a female. Walking into solid objects was a very frequent occurrence! One category always walked as if they were carrying a huge weight on their shoulders. They believed that walking with a stoop was a sign of humility; other people thought they were just plain stupid.

One group of Pharisees kept a diary of their good deeds and used this as a sort of bargaining account with God. Perhaps it went something like: 'God, I've done three good deeds this week and now it's my turn, OK?' Another category were those Pharisees who believed that at any moment God would get really angry with them and so they went around continually looking behind them (that category is the 'Timid' Pharisees). And finally, there were those Pharisees who genuinely believed that doing acts of charity and being honest with God was the best way to follow and worship God.

So, when some Pharisees came to Jesus and warned him of Herod's threat to kill him, it could have been difficult to try and guess what the Pharisees were up to. Were they really concerned about the threat to Jesus, or did they think they were doing a good deed by warning him? Did it count as a 'tick' in the 'act of kindness' box, or did they see Herod's threat as part of God's anger for some reason? Jesus could have spent all day trying to sort out why, and for whose benefit, these Pharisees had come to warn him. But rather than waste time, he decided that he had a task to complete and nothing was going to stop him. Even though Jesus knew for certain that he was going to his death, he was determined to do things his way (which was God's way) and it didn't matter what people might say or do.

Remind the group of the game they played at the beginning of the session. Discuss some of the following questions:

- How did they feel during the game? Angry, amused, or totally bewildered?
- Did the game seem pointless?
- What did they think of the role they were asked to perform (Grabber, Giver or Goodie)?
- Did they feel like changing roles at any time? Why?

Can the group think of any circumstances or situations that compare with the game? For instance, do they know people who are always on the take? Or people who give their time or money for charity? Can the game help us understand the feelings of other people?

Ask the group to suggest words which indicate how they felt during the game. Whether they felt awkward, daft, annoyed, puzzled or frustrated, each of these words can make us question what we believe we should be doing. Write the words onto a flipchart.

(Allow 5 minutes.)

Place the flipchart in the centre of the room or cut the words out and stick them around the room. Ask the group to think about any situation or problem where they feel unable to do what they believe is the right thing. While the group are quiet, read the following:

Proverbs 3:1-6.
My child, remember my teachings and instructions
 and obey them completely.
They will help you live a long and prosperous life.
Let love and loyalty always show like a necklace,
 and write them in your mind.
God and people will like you and consider you a success.
With all your heart you must trust the Lord
 and not in your own judgement.
Always let him lead you,
 and he will clear the road for you to follow.

THE WRINKLIES GET UPSET

Characters The ever-lovely Old 1 and Old 2, feeling at odds with everybody.

Scene The aged grumps are sitting on a bench in the market place.

Props bench
knotted hankies for grumps' heads
pair of walking sticks

Old 1 It really puts you off your pork scratchings, it does.

Old 2 What does?

Old 1 *(Points in front with walking stick)* That.

Old 2 *(Squints to see what Old 1 is pointing at)* Can't see much.

Old 1 Tell me something I don't know.

Old 2 Oooh! Who's rubbed your fur the wrong way?

Old 1 Them *(points stick again*) and now you.

Old 2 Perhaps we should start again.

Old 1 Start again? Are you mad?

Old 2 Well, at least I might grasp what's putting you off your food.

Old 1 I wouldn't want to start out all over again. I don't reckon I could put up with being young again.

Old 2 What on earth are you going on about?

Old 1 Being young again. What a waste of perfectly good health. The young kids today, I ask you. All that energy and vitality going to waste. They run around like headless chickens and wonder why they get into all sorts of trouble.

Old 2 You were young once.

Old 1 Sssh! *(Puts finger to lips)* Sssh! You never know who's listening. That's how rumours start.

Old 2 *(Points to knotted hanky on Old 1's head)* I don't think that's doing its job. Letting a bit too much sun in.

Old 1 *(Pats head)* Nothing wrong with my head, which is more than can be said for that lot. *(Points again)*

Old 2 *(Puts hands flat against face)* Here we go again. All right, who? what? why?

Old 1 I can't be doing with all that do-gooding.

Old 2 Don't knock it, a little bit of help here and there benefits everyone.

Old 1 Not the way they go about it. The only people who benefit are themselves. It's like a circus.

Old 2 How do you make that out?

Old 1 Bunch of clowns, that's what.

Old 2 Look, for all the uninitiated psychopaths out there, please explain what you're going on about.

Old 1 Simple.

Old 2 *(Tuts)* You're telling me.

Old 1 I would be if you didn't keep interrupting.

Old 2 Well, get on with it, then.

Old 1 I'm trying to but a wizened old fool keeps rattling his gums.

Old 2 *(Waves walking stick in front of Old 1's face)* I can think of other uses for this, you know.

Old 1 *(Groans and holds chin)* Ow, ooh, aah.

Old 2 I didn't touch you.

Old 1 You're not quick enough to put your fingers in wet paint. It's me gums, playing up something rotten.

Old 2 That'll teach you to visit that back-street dentist.

Old 1 Old Cubbing reckons that dentist is the best in the business.

Old 2 He is. His reputation is unrivalled.

Old 1 There you go, then.

Old 2 Unrivalled as a stone mason.

Old 1 *(Holds chin again and groans)* Ow, it's almost as bad as watching those hypocrites pretending they're doing some-one a good turn.

Old 2 Leave them alone. They're not doing any harm.

Old 1 That's where you're wrong. You can't trust 'em. You never know where you are with them.

Old 2 If they're going to help you out of a spot of difficulty, what's the problem?

Old 1 *(Shakes head)* Some folk never learn. Look, if someone is going to help, fine, OK. Just leave it at that and get on with your life.

Old 2 So what's your problem?

Old 1 Those do-gooders who should just help and then disappear, quietly.

Old 2 They don't?

Old 1 Disappear? That's the last thing they do. You can always tell when they've inflicted their help on some poor unsuspecting individual. They rarely help if there isn't a crowd to witness their charity or add their endeavour to a list of good deeds that they read with a sense of glowing pride.

Old 2 You're not very keen on these people, are you?

Old 1 Too right. I can't stand the constant reminders of their meddling in my state of desperation. Drama merchants the lot of them.

Old 2 Not a bit like you.

Old 1 Definitely not. You won't catch me sticking my nose where it's not wanted.

Old 2 Never! You spend so long moaning about having to do anything that someone else has done the necessary long before you get there.

Old 1 I wouldn't deprive someone of their opportunity to show a little kindness.

Old 2 Hmm.

TODAY'S SPECIAL

You what?

Luke 13:1-9: Turn back to God

Equipment:
Lego or similar building blocks
wastepaper basket
pens and paper
music and lyrics

Divide the group into three or four teams. Give each team a box of building blocks and tell them that their task is to build a tower which will be strong enough to support a wastepaper basket (full or empty, it depends how tough you want to make the game). Before the game begins, choose one member from each team and ask them to behave as a saboteur in the building process. You might like to choose and brief the saboteurs before the session begins. The saboteurs are to make a nuisance of themselves by giving conflicting advice, knocking blocks over and causing as much hassle as they can. Advise the saboteurs that their behaviour should be planned carefully so as not to seem too obstructive, but enough to make it awkward for their team to complete the task.

After two minutes 'test' each construction with the wastepaper basket. It might help the saboteurs if you let the other team members in on the 'plot' to obstruct the building process.

Did any of the teams guess what the saboteurs were doing or did they genuinely think that the saboteurs were being a *real* 'pain'?

(Allow 10 minutes for this activity.)

We are often shocked by people's actions and left wondering why they behave the way they do.

Have a look at 'Beauty for brokenness' by Graham Kendrick (*The source*, 37), or 'Have you heard the good news' by Stuart Garrard (*The source*, 146).

(Allow approximately 5 minutes for this.)

Hardly a day goes by without some news which shocks us and causes us to question someone's behaviour.

Read Luke 13:1-9.
Jesus is brought news of an atrocity carried out by the Roman soldiers acting on the orders of Pilate. It was almost as if he were being asked, 'How much more evidence to you need before you condemn the Romans for what they do?'

To the Jews, the whole concept of the 'Messiah' or 'Saviour' was that God would establish his kingdom on earth. Many believed that Jesus was going to force the Romans out of Israel and a new order, or government, would take their place. The Essenes, in particular, trained for the day when God's kingdom would be established by force. Another collection of groups was known as the Zealots, who thought that God might need a bit of a hand when it came to sorting out the Romans. Several other small groups existed, including one called the Sicarii (dagger men), who carried out assassinations and really wound the Roman authorities up.

So the people were expecting Jesus to say, 'Yeah, let's give those Romans a real hiding'. Instead of inciting them to action, Jesus suggested that the people look at the situation from another perspective. Firstly, he wanted everyone to understand that the people who had been killed were not being punished by God for being dodgy characters. And secondly, he wanted to get across the idea that everyone is capable of behaving in a way or committing acts that some other people would find horrifying.

In Luke 13:5, Jesus puts forward the view that the people should hate the sin, or crime, but not hate the person involved. The story of the fig tree is one way of suggesting that we need to be patient and give a person time to regret what they've done and turn to God. Forgiveness is an easy word to say but an extremely difficult thing to do. Jesus is warning against creating a 'goodies' and 'baddies' list because everyone is capable of doing the wrong thing. Change is a heart attitude and not an act of revenge.

Ask the group if they have heard of any news or events recently which have made them feel angry or powerless. Discuss some of the atrocities or natural disasters which have occurred in various parts of the world.

- What do the group feel about these situations?
- Is anyone to blame?
- What should happen to the people involved?

Discuss some local or personal issues which cause the group to feel similar emotions to those provoked by what they've just discussed. Why did these events happen? Could they have been avoided?

Give each member of the group a piece of paper and a pen. Ask each of them to write a sentence or two about a situation which they feel strongly about or one in which they may have been involved. When they have finished, fold the pieces of paper and place them in a pile in the centre of the room.

(Allow 5 minutes.)

Suggest to the group that they should now spend a few moments thinking about the situation they've just written on the paper. While they are quiet, read the following prayer:

Lord,
I've gone through every emotion in the dictionary.
I've shouted until my throat hurts.
My head aches with the thoughts
 of senseless violence,
 of mindless actions
 that have robbed people
 of their hopes, their dreams, their lives.
I can't pretend to understand
 or find an answer
 to the jigsaw of events
 that froze a moment in time
 for ever.
Tears sometimes say more
 than mere words can express.
A cry from the heart
 speaks more wisdom
 than a thousand wise men.
But all I can say is
 I don't understand, Lord.
All I can pray is
 that somehow,
 for all those involved,
 you would bring peace
 and understanding,
 while I place my life
 in your hands.
Keep me safe, keep me willing
 to hear your voice and your heart.

TODAY'S SPECIAL

So what are you gonna do?

Luke 15:1-3,11-32: Two sons

Equipment:
large cardboard box
four or five smaller boxes
tape, glue and paper-clips
straws, pipe-cleaners, bamboo canes and thin wire
toy car or ball
stones
basket
flipchart
music and lyrics

Divide the group into four or five teams. Place the large box in the centre of the room. Arrange the smaller boxes in a circle with the large box in the centre. Each team is given a collection of tape, glue, paper-clips, straws, pipe-cleaners, canes and wire. The object is to build a bridge from the smaller box across to the large box in the centre (the distance between the large box and smaller ones depends on the space available and how difficult you want to make the task).

The winning team is the one whose bridge can support the toy car or the ball as it travels from the small box to the large box.

- How did the groups organise themselves?
- Were they successful?
- Why?
- What problems occurred?

(Allow 10 minutes for this activity.)

Building bridges offers a lot of insights into individual and group behaviour.

Take a look at 'Oh, I was made for this' by Graham Kendrick (*The source*, 389) or 'Did you feel the mountains tremble?' by Martin Smith (*The source*, 80). Alternatively, you might like to use the drama sketch *The Wrinklies hear some gossip* (see page 86).

(Allow approximately 5 minutes for this.)

Building bridges takes a lot of effort and can often prove to be more difficult than we ever imagined.

Read Luke 15:1-3, 11-32.

Jesus gives us a story-line any soap opera would be proud of. Under Jewish law the eldest son was entitled to two thirds of his father's property and the youngest son was given a third. Sometimes the father could give his sons their inheritance early if he wanted to retire from running his affairs and take it easy. But in this instance, the younger son actually says, 'I wish you were dead'. Things must have been pretty rough for the son to feel like this. Perhaps, as the younger son, he felt he wasn't given enough respect or responsibility. He might even have been jealous of the fact that his elder brother was going to get twice as much of the inheritance as he was. There are many reasons why families argue, fall out and say things they later wish they hadn't.

In the story, the young son allowed the money to slip through his hands and he was left hoping that the pigs would leave him a few crumbs to eat. For a Jew, the pig was about as welcome as a chocolate gâteau at a weight-watchers' convention.

The younger son soon realised that he had lost more than he had ever gained by turning his back on his father and decided to go home and ask to become one of his father's farm workers. As soon as his father saw him coming, he ran to meet him (the father running from his property to greet his son wasn't a normal action in Jewish society).

Once back home the young son was treated far differently from what he had expected. He was given a robe, which meant the same as giving someone honour and respect. Then he was given a ring, which signified authority. Next he was given shoes, which were a symbol of freedom and finally, a feast was prepared. Father and son were reconciled, brought back together, not back to where they were when the argument began, but to a new place, a position where the son was given more than he could ever hope for.

In contrast, the elder brother lost the plot completely. He was annoyed at his father's actions, and refused to be reconciled to his brother. Everyone within the family had been affected by the young son's actions but the father had chosen to welcome his son back with open arms. Perhaps if the father (God) decides to throw a party we should all take part in the celebration and not question his judgement. In other words, if God forgives, who are we to argue?

Ask the group to suggest situations that they've experienced where arguments have caused people to feel separated from those they once felt close to.

- How did it happen?
- What were the causes?
- Have the people concerned dealt with the problem?
- How was it resolved?

You might have to be sensitive to some of the issues or the fact that some of the group may feel too awkward or shy to talk personally. It may prove easier to discuss ways of avoiding conflict within a group or family. Ask group members to suggest a list of recommended actions or behaviour which either avoid conflict or bring people back together.

(Allow 5 minutes.)

Give each of the group members a small pebble or stone. Ask them to think of someone close to them who is experiencing a problem within their family. Place a basket in the centre of the room and after the group have spent a few moments in thought, ask them to place the stone in the basket. The collected stones represent everyone who is having a difficult time at the moment. If the group agree, you might like to write names or initials of the people involved on a piece of paper and place them on a notice board as a prayer reminder.

While everyone is quiet, read the following prayer:

Lord,
it's often difficult
to know who's right and who's wrong.
Just as it takes two to argue,
it takes two to agree
to build the bridge
which will join two islands
that have been separated
by an ocean of misunderstanding.
Please help us to learn
how to build bridges,
no matter how far
or how wide
the gap.

Help us to be willing
to realise the loneliness
of anger, of hurt and of damaged pride,
so that we can be a continent of hope
and not a cluster of islands in a raging sea.

THE WRINKLIES HEAR SOME GOSSIP

Characters The two grumps who enjoy nothing better than a good gossip.

Scene The two aged grumps are leaning against a wall, chatting about a new piece of juicy gossip.

Props pair of walking sticks
threadbare jackets
pack of fish-paste sandwiches

Old 1 Did you hear about old man Jennings?

Old 2 Old man Jennings? He's not been chasing dogs again, has he?

Old 1 Not since the vet gave him a dose of some foul smelling, sticky green liquid. No, I got the latest from Ma Smith at the bakery yesterday morning.

Old 2 Fresh from the bakers, you might say?

Old 1 *(Leans on walking stick)* Yep, nothing better than a crusty loaf with juicy gossip filling.

Old 2 *(Licks lips)* Nothing better, I'd say.

Old 1 *(Sniffs as if smelling freshly baked bread)* Hmmm.

Old 2 Well?

Old 1 Well what? *(Offers Old 2 a fish-paste sandwich)* Fancy a bite?

Old 2 Ta. *(Takes sandwich)* Now, Ma Smith.

Old 1 What about her?

Old 2 You tell me.

Old 1 Haven't heard anything about her since that escapade with the camel and the candle.

Old 2 That was a real laugh. Kept the local gossip mafia occupied for months. So, what was it that she told you?

Old 1 *(Takes bite of sandwich)* Told me?

Old 2 Well, it wasn't me buying the crusty loaf.

Old 1 *(Scratches head)* Oh, I remember, old man Jennings.

Old 2 I'm listening.

Old 1 So was half of the shop, so the news will have spread quicker than a sneeze. Anyway, it concerns young Jennings.

Old 2 Young Jennings or young, young Jennings?

Old 1 You developing a stutter?

Old 2 The only thing I'll develop is pneumonia if you don't get on with it.

Old 1 OK, don't rush me.

Old 2 The nearest you'll ever get to rushing is falling asleep.

Old 1 Merely resting my eyes. They need the rest, I've had 'em a long time.

Old 2 And mine are ageing by the second. I suppose you're going to tell me about young, young Jennings coming home from his travels?

Old 1 *(Tuts)* Why didn't you tell me you already knew?

Old 2 Wouldn't want to spoil the moment. Besides, you took so long trying to tell me what Ma Smith had said, my mind wandered.

Old 1	That went walkabout years ago. At least young, young Jennings came back.
Old 2	I'll ignore that comment. I heard that old man Jennings was putting some rubbish in the bin when he saw his son shuffling along the road.
Old 1	Must have come as a bit of a shock!
Old 2	Shock? I'd have given the lad a shock, I'd have throttled him.
Old 1	It's a good job you're not his dad then.
Old 2	Young 'uns today, want everything and the kitchen sink before they're barely able to walk.
Old 1	Lad broke his mother's heart when he left.
Old 2	Not surprising, she thought the world of that sink.
Old 1	Yeah, shame.
Old 2	You're telling me. The lad took everything he could lay his hands on, wasted the lot and came back empty handed.
Old 1	Ma Smith reckons the lad went wild.
Old 2	I'd have gone wild if it'd been my lad.
Old 1	Old man Jennings welcomed the lad back with open arms, apparently.
Old 2	How daft can you get?
Old 1	You think that's daft? Old man Jennings not only welcomed the lad back, he got everyone running around to prepare a slap-up meal for the lad.
Old 2	I heard that. The lad came back with more holes in his clothes than a fishing net.

Old 1 That's nothing new nowadays. My lad reckons it's fashion.

Old 2 I'll give 'em fashion. Ungrateful, I call it. Walking around like an unkept garden nobody cared for.

Old 1 Times change.

Old 2 It's not times they need to change, it's their socks.

Old 1 True. Still, at least old man Jennings had the sense to give the lad a coat to cover up the disgraceful display of tatters and stench.

Old 2 I bet young Jennings wasn't impressed.

Old 1 Too right. As the eldest son, he stayed at home and did as he was told. Got on with the ditch digging, putting fences up, cleaning out the goats and taking the sheep to market every Thursday.

Old 2 Reckon old man Jennings was a bit of a slave driver myself.

Old 1 Reckon you're right there. No wonder young, young Jennings left home.

Old 2 No wonder. I'd have done the same. Any sandwiches left?

TODAY'S SPECIAL

What's that smell?

John 12:1-8: At Bethany.

Equipment:
range of small bottles
various coloured liquids
flipchart
music and lyrics

Pour the liquids into the bottles. Try using a variety of liquids which have a distinctive smell, e.g. disinfectant, perfume, tea, coffee, orange, water. You might like to make some of the 'aromas' more interesting by adding some noxious as well as pleasant smells!

Organise a number of volunteers from the group and blindfold each of them. One by one arrange for each volunteer to smell the liquids and ask them to guess what is contained within each bottle. As a special treat, ask each volunteer for a number (if there are eight bottles, numbers between 1 and 8). Whichever number they choose, they are allowed to have a drop of the liquid from the chosen bottle placed behind their ear!

(Allow 10 minutes for this activity.)

Apprehension and sometimes annoyance can often blind us to seeing what is really in front of our noses.

Have a look at 'You laid aside your majesty' by Noel Richards (*The source*, 601) or 'At your feet we fall' by David Fellingham (*The source*, 35).

(Allow approximately 5 minutes for this.)

It's only too easy to think that who we are and what we have isn't worth a great deal.

Read John 12:1-8.
Jesus had gone to Bethany, to the house of Simon the Leper, for a meal. Martha, Mary and Lazarus were most likely the children of Simon. The meal was to be a leisurely dinner, a time to enjoy eating, drinking and good company.

The meal had been prepared especially for Jesus after his extremely busy time teaching and healing all around the area. The sight of Lazarus at the table would have made the meal a special occasion. Lazarus (formerly known as dead Lazarus!) was a close friend and Jesus must have taken real pleasure in raising him from the dead.

Everyone would have known that the meal was a special occasion but not everyone would have been able to say why it was so special. Jesus knew that these were his last few days of freedom and being with his disciples and close friends would have been particularly important for him. The disciples would have known that things were 'hotting up' but even they might not have been able to say precisely what was going to happen. To Mary, Martha and Lazarus it was enough to have their close friend spend some time with them.

Martha seems to have been the practical person, the one who knew how to make people feel comfortable and catered for. She offered her skills in the kitchen as an expression of her love towards Jesus. Mary expressed her love in a different way.

The washing of feet was a normal courtesy before a meal. Mary's actions were significant for three reasons. First, the perfume that Mary poured on Jesus' feet was expensive and quite probably irreplaceable, given the cost. Second, it was usually traditional, and a sign of honour, to use oil or perfume to anoint someone's head. By anointing Jesus' feet Mary was showing her humility by not claiming the honour of anointing Jesus' head. And third, Mary wiped Jesus' feet with her hair. At the time, no respectable woman would appear in public with her hair loose. By using her hair to wipe his feet of Jesus, Mary was setting aside tradition and respectability in her desire to express her love for Jesus, regardless of what people thought of her.

In their different ways both Mary and Martha gave Jesus an expression of their love. No one objected to Martha's gift of food as everyone would have shared in the meal and enjoyed the food. Mary's gift was personal and only for Jesus.

We each have our own, individual ways of expressing how we feel and what we consider precious. Every expression is relevant and special. Just because some acts are highly visible and make an impact immediately doesn't mean that other forms of expression are less important or meaningful. Each of us is unique and important to God. The most important thing is the expression of our hearts, not what other people think of us.

Ask the group to think of the things that other people do for them which help make their lives comfortable, happy or bearable. Write some of the comments on the flipchart. What about some of the things people do that we take for granted, e.g washing clothes, tidying bedrooms, preparing meals? List all the ways in which people contribute to our daily lives. Now, turn the question around and ask the group to consider ways in which they contribute to other people's well-being. Underline the actions which come into both categories – ways in which the group members both give and receive.

(Allow 5 minutes.)

Place the flipchart in the centre of the room and ask the group to think about some of the ways in which people help them. While the group are quiet, read the following prayer:

Lord,
   you'll have to speak up,
   I can't hear you very well.
The sound of my own voice
   is almost deafening
   with a dustbin
   over my head.
It's not the best place to be,
   underneath a container for rubbish.
But perhaps it's the best place
   for the dustbin.
I wasn't pushed,
   I didn't stumble or trip.
I'm sitting here
   by choice
   because it's how I feel
   about myself.
Excuse me,
   what was that you said?
You want to come and join me?
Surely you can find a better place to be.
Pardon?
You can't think of anywhere better
   than here with me?
Hang on a minute, I'm coming out.
There's not enough room for two
   and anyway, I feel much better now there's you and me.

TODAY'S SPECIAL

A bit of a do

Luke 22:14-23: The Lord's Supper

Equipment:
pack of playing cards
bread and wine/juice
music and lyrics

Select sufficient cards for each member of the group to have *one* card. Make sure you include either the Queen of Clubs or the Queen of Spades, but not both. Shuffle the cards and distribute one card to each member of the group. The group must not show their card to any other member of the group. The game is simple. The holder of the black queen has to eliminate the other members of the group by winking at them once. The person winked at counts to ten, then places their card in front of them and say 'I'm out'. They must not identify the person who winked at them. If a member of the group thinks they know who's 'winking' then they are allowed to accuse them. If they are wrong, the accuser is out of the game. The game continues until everyone is 'out' or the eliminator is discovered.

(Allow 10 minutes for this activity.)

It's infuriating trying to sort out the innocent and the guilty.

Take a look at 'We do not presume' by Andy Piercy (*The source*, 545) or 'Here is bread' by Graham Kendrick (*The source*, 163).

(Allow approximately 5 minutes for this.)

Another meal but this time the mood is sombre.

Read Luke 22:14-23.

The Passover meal was a celebration of the release of the Israelites from slavery in Egypt (see Exodus 12-13). Jesus brought his disciples together to share in his last Passover meal, which the disciples understood was a special meal because everyone in Jerusalem, and many visitors to the city, celebrated the Passover. For Jesus, this meal held more significance than the disciples appreciated.

The relationship between Jesus and the religious authorities had become tense. He had challenged their traditions and thinking and they were worried he was becoming too popular. The disciples were also aware of the tension but they seemed confident that Jesus had everything under control. Jesus did have everything under control, but not in the way the disciples thought.

On the night of the original 'Passover' the angel of death killed every first-born son but *passed over* the homes where the lintels of the doors had been smeared with the blood of a lamb. Jesus had already been referred to as the 'Lamb of God' (see John 1:29).

During his meal with the disciples, Jesus took the unleavened bread (made without yeast as a reminder of how the Israelites had to escape from Egypt as quickly as possible – there hadn't been any time to wait for the dough to rise). The bread was a symbol, recalling a significant event. Jesus took the bread, broke it and told his disciples that the bread represented his body, to be broken as a sacrifice. Next, Jesus took the wine, another symbol, and drank it. The wine was to act as a reminder of Jesus' blood, which again represented a sacrifice.

The death and sacrifice of Jesus was the only way in which a relationship with God could be restored. The symbols of the bread and the wine are constant reminders that we have continuous access to God because of the sacrifice of Jesus.

Place the bread and the wine/juice on a table in front of the group. Can the group think of other symbols that remind us of events or special occasions? – e.g cross, dove, fish. Discuss the importance of symbols.

- Why do we need symbols?
- Would we forget without symbols to remind us?

(Allow 5 minutes.)

Leave the bread and the wine/juice on the table and ask the group to be quiet while you read the following:

Psalm 107:1-9.
Shout praises to the Lord!
He is good to us, and his love never fails.
Everyone the Lord has rescued from trouble
  should praise him.
Everyone he has brought from the east and the west,
  the north and the south.
Some of you were lost in the scorching desert,
  far from a town.

PALM SUNDAY

You were hungry and thirsty and about to give up.
You were in serious trouble,
   but you prayed to the Lord, and he rescued you.
Straight away he brought you to a town.
You should praise the Lord for his love
   and for the wonderful things he does for all of us.
To everyone who is thirsty, he gives something to drink;
   to everyone who is hungry
   he gives good things to eat.

TODAY'S SPECIAL

You must be seeing things!

Luke 24:1-12: Jesus is alive

Equipment:
flipchart
glue or tacks
assorted pictures
pens and paper
seed from a plant
music and lyrics

Select a variety of pictures taken from a wide range of magazines and/or newspapers. Cut out a portion of the picture so that the image is incomplete (remember to keep a note of what the picture was originally). Stick/glue the images onto the flipchart and number each image.

Distribute the pens and paper to the group and ask them to guess what the original picture was. The person with the most correct answers is the winner.

(Allow 10 minutes for this activity.)

Images are open to our interpretation. It isn't always as easy as we think to identify even familiar images from a small portion or a strange angle.

Have a look at 'I will love you for the cross' by Matt Redman and Beth Vickers (*Re:source 2000*, 6) or 'Nothing shall separate us' by Noel and Tricia Richards (*The source*, 377).

(Allow approximately 5 minutes.)

Newspapers thrive on reports of strange sightings and unexplained phenomena.

Read Luke 24:1-12.
It was extremely early on Sunday morning. It was still dark although the sun was just starting to signal its arrival for the day. Mary and several other women went to the tomb of Jesus to complete the last functions of the burial ceremony. The spices they took with them would have been a mixture of myrrh and aloes which acted as a sort of disinfectant and deodorant. It would have been a very sad occasion for the women. After three hectic yet incredible years, where Jesus had literally changed

people's lives, the end had come. The final act of putting spices on the dead body was almost like closing a book; it was finished.

Jesus had used these very same words a couple of days earlier as he had hung on the cross: 'It is finished.' But his idea of 'finished' was very different from that of the women who came to his tomb. What Jesus had struggled for and eventually died for was finished. Stage One was complete and now Stage Two was about to begin.

When the women arrived at the tomb, the heavy circular stone had been moved, the tomb was open. Inside the tomb, the body had vanished. Various questions must have gone through the women's minds. What could have happened? Who could have taken the body? The women's thoughts were occupied with the practical side of things: who, what, where? They'd seen Jesus die – that was it, over and done.

In the gloom two men appeared. Their clothes shone in the darkness. The sight must have been frightening. The women were already concerned about the loss of the body and now here was something else to think about. The response from the two men was incredible. Why were the women looking where dead people were buried? Well, what else are you supposed to find in a graveyard? Then the amazing statement: 'Jesus isn't here, he's alive!'

The women ran back to the disciples and told them what they had and *hadn't* seen. The Greek word, which the disciples used to describe the women's report is one more often used by ancient Greek doctors to define someone who is 'babbling', someone who has a fever or is insane. The women's mixture of amazement and excitement didn't seem to make any impression on the disciples who must have been more interested in what was for breakfast.

Only Peter, who had denied Jesus three times, had the courage to check the story out. He also returned confused and wondering what had happened. Now it wasn't so much who had done it, but why?

Ask the group what words they think would describe the thoughts and feelings of the women when they went to the tomb of Jesus. Write them up on the flipchart. Then ask them for words to describe the thoughts and feelings of the disciples after the women had come back with their report.

- Do any of these words describe our thoughts or the way we feel about God, Jesus, the Holy Spirit?
- Is there a problem with us having these kinds of thoughts?
- If even the people who had known Jesus well could feel that way, then isn't it only reasonable for us to have the same thoughts and feelings whenever we try to understand what God wants with us?

(Allow 5 minutes.)

Place the seed on a table where everybody can see it. Can anyone identify the plant from the seed? With difficulty or not at all! Only when the plant becomes established can we really be certain what it is and what we can use it for. We have to be patient.

Our life is similar to the seed. Where we are going and what we are going to do in the future are questions we would all like to know the answers to. It's possibly a good job that we can't always! We need to trust that God knows what he's doing.

Ask the group to be quiet while you read the following:

Psalm 62:5-8.
Only God gives inward peace, and I depend on him.
God alone is the mighty rock that keeps me safe,
and he is the fortress where I feel secure.
God saves me and honours me.
He is that mighty rock where I find safety.
Trust God, my friends,
and always tell him each one of your concerns.
God is our place of safety.

TODAY'S SPECIAL

Lock that door!

John 20:19-31: Jesus appears to his disciples

Equipment:
card
pen and paper
candle
music and lyrics

You will need an even number of pieces of card. On one piece of card draw a series of interlocking shapes, similar to a puzzle. Copy the 'puzzle' onto a second card. Taking another card, draw a different 'puzzle' and again copy the 'puzzle' onto another piece of card. Repeat the process until you have used all the cards. On the 'original' set of cards, cut out the interlocking shapes leaving a completed copy for each 'puzzle'.

Divide the group into pairs. Have the pairs sit back to back so that they cannot see each other's 'puzzle'. One of the partners has the copy of the 'puzzle' while the other has the cut out pieces. The partner with the copy 'puzzle' tries to describe each piece of the 'puzzle' and where to place it.

What difficulties did the group have completing the 'puzzles'?

(Allow 10 minutes for this activity.)

During the previous activity some feelings of confusion may have crept into the proceedings!

Take a look at 'I'm learning to love you' by Paul Oakley (*Re:source 2000*, 4) or 'Though I feel afraid' by Ian White (*The source*, 522).

(Allow approximately 5 minutes.)

Feelings of confusion and fear often make a situation appear hopeless.

Read John 20:19-31.
It had been a horrendous few days for the disciples. Everything they had believed in and hoped for appeared to have gone for ever. All sorts of rumours were doing the rounds about what had happened to Jesus and what would happen to the disciples if the Jewish leaders got hold of them!

Confusion was the flavour of the day as the disciples gathered together in a room. Fear of being caught by the authorities drove them to lock the door. So many different thoughts must have been going through their minds. Why had the people suddenly turned against them? What more did Jesus have to do to prove who he was? What would happen to the disciples now? Where could they go? Was it possible for them to return to their former jobs and carry on as if nothing had happened? Questions, questions, fear and confusion, but no answers.

The feelings of dejection and hopelessness must have coloured their thoughts. Each of the disciples had experienced so much and seen so many amazing things happen that they must have been wishing for a miracle.

They hardly had time to blink before Jesus appeared in the middle of the room. The disciples probably thought that they'd all gone completely bonkers. This couldn't be happening, could it?

Jesus approached them with an everyday greeting: 'Peace be to you.' This carried a more significant meaning than simply 'I hope you don't get into trouble'! – although keeping out of trouble must have been just what the disciples wanted. The greeting means: 'May God give you every good thing.'

The disciples may have been a bit sceptical at first. You can imagine their first reaction to be: 'Yeah, we could do with a few good things, like how to get the authorities of our backs', but their scepticism was short-lived after Jesus had showed them his hands and side. The disciples may still have felt a little confused but at least they didn't feel as if they were on their own any more.

Although Jesus had explained to the disciples what was going to happen, when things began to get tough the disciples couldn't help feeling confused and frightened. Jesus had promised that he wouldn't just leave them to get on with life on their own.

It's never easy to feel confident when situations get a bit sticky. All too often we can feel as if we're up to our necks in it and completely on our own. But Jesus has given his word that he will never leave us to try and sort things out by ourselves. It may take some believing, but it's true.

Give each member of the group a pen and piece of paper. Ask them to think of situations or circumstances which have made them feel confused and/or afraid, or still do. You might like to start by sharing something that makes you feel uncomfortable.

When the group have completed writing on their pieces of paper, ask them to fold the paper into a small square and place it at the base of the candle which you have placed in the centre of the room.

(Allow 5 minutes.)

Ask the group to be quiet as you light the candle. While everyone is quiet, read the following prayer:

Lord,
at times –
well, if I'm honest, quite a lot of the time –
I feel as if my head
is in a blender.
My thoughts whizz around,
until everything
is in a complete mess.
It makes my stomach churn,
and my legs feel odd.
If I could close my eyes,
stick my fingers in my ears
and scream,
then I would, if it made
any difference
to the way I feel.
You may have noticed
that when I tried that last time
people gave me funny looks
and wondered
if I was quite right in the head.
I couldn't admit to them
that my head felt full of spaghetti
and if I had told them
it wouldn't have made any difference.
But telling you how I feel
seems to make all the difference.
Thank goodness for that.

TODAY'S SPECIAL

I'm not sure about this

Acts 9:1-20: Saul becomes a follower of the Lord

Equipment:
sheets of paper
pens
music and lyrics

Give each member of the group a pen and piece of paper. Ask them to draw a line down the centre of the page. On the left-hand side of the paper they write down all those characteristics which they feel are good qualities in a friend, and on the right-hand side of the page all those characteristics which they don't consider to be positive qualities in a friend.

Once the group have completed this activity individually, ask them to form small groups of two or three members and compile a short list of the qualities that they feel a friend should have.

Now, as a whole group, try to define what 'friendship' really is.

(Allow 10 minutes for this activity.)

A friendship is not always an easy relationship. There needs to be a lot of understanding, compromise and a willingness to laugh at yourself.

Take a look at 'What a friend I've found' by Martin Smith (*The source*, 565) or 'We must work together' by Ian Mizen and Andy Pressdee (*The source*, 553).

(Allow approximately 5 minutes.)

Sometimes friendships have a funny way of starting out.

Read Acts 9:1-20.

Saul, later known as Paul, had recently acted as a sort of coat-rack for a group of Jews (members of the Sanhedrin, a Jewish court or council) who handed Saul their outer clothes while they stoned a bloke named Stephen to death (see Acts 7:54-60). Saul thought that anyone who believed in Jesus was an absolute and complete heretic and deserved everything that could be thrown at them. A short while later Saul had written permission from the High Priest to 'bury' these 'believers in Jesus' under as much rubble as he could find. So he set off for Jerusalem with a few mates, intent on sorting out the troublemakers.

Approaching Damascus, Saul got the interrogation treatment by God as a bright light blinded him and left his mates speechless. The same eyes that had watched Stephen being stoned now couldn't see to throw a plum stone. Someone took pity on Saul and led him to Damascus where he sat for three days without food or drink.

In the meantime, God had spoken to a bloke called Ananias who also lived in Damascus. Ananias was willing to go wherever God sent him – that was until God told him where he wanted him to go and whom he was to see!

Ananias couldn't believe his ears. God asked him to go and speak to someone who made alligators appear charming. Ananias complained and tried to remind God just who Saul was. God was having none of it and told Ananias to get on with the job.

As soon as Ananias did as God had asked something like fish scales fell from Saul's eyes and he was able to see again. Not only was Saul able to see the physical things around him, he was also able to 'see' (understand) that Jesus was who he claimed to be: the Son of God.

Even though he wasn't confident about what God had asked him to do, Ananias acted in friendship towards Saul by placing his hands on Saul. The placing of hands, usually on the shoulders or head, was a gesture of acceptance and recognition.

Such was the power of this expression of acceptance that a few days later Saul was preaching that Jesus was the Son of God. Saul's preaching was so effective that it wasn't long before the very people who had encouraged Saul to kill the followers of Jesus, were planning to kill Saul. At least now Saul knew who his friends were.

Ask each person to look again at their lists of characteristics of friends they produced earlier and highlight those characteristics (good and not so good, be honest) they think apply to them.

Ask the group to consider the question 'Why do we need friends?' Are there any situations or circumstances where it would be easier if we were left on our own?'

Allow each group member to respond honestly even if their viewpoint differs from the rest of the group.

(Allow 5 minutes.)

Suggest to the group that it might be appropriate to spend a few moments thinking about friends and how they, as individuals, can be friends to other people. While they are quiet, read the following:

Ecclesiastes 4:9-10.
You are better off having a friend than being all alone, because then you will get more enjoyment out of what you earn. If you fall, your friend can help you up. But if you fall without having a friend nearby, you are really in trouble.

TODAY'S SPECIAL

Time to get up

Acts 9:36-43: Peter brings Tabitha back to life

Equipment:
paper and pens
candles
flipchart
music and lyrics

Give each group member a piece of paper and a pen. Ask them to think about what they would write on their own headstone. For example: 'I kept telling them I was ill' or 'Back in five minutes' or even 'I'll be lucky to get out of this alive'. Suggest to your group that they might like to think of epitaphs that say something either about what they would like to have achieved or about their personality.

Have a chat about how group members would like to be remembered. Are there any specific things they would like to do, or see done, before they die?

(Allow 10 minutes for this activity.)

Although the idea of death might be 'something that happens to other people', and it seems there is a lifetime of experience to cram into our existence, the effects of death are constantly around us.

Have a look at 'In every circumstance' by David Fellingham (*The source*, 227) or 'Can we walk upon the water' by Matt Redman (*The source*, 64).

(Allow approximately 5 minutes.)

It's not being morbid to recognise that at some point we might have difficulty outliving our own funeral. But we already know our beginning, and rather than concentrate on the ending, there's a whole big chunk in the middle to get to grips with.

Read Acts 9:36-43.

At Joppa, a coastal town, a community of Christians was mourning the death of a woman named Tabitha. She was well known for going out of her way to help people who were less fortunate than she was.

From the description of her death (verse 39), many widows were crying at the loss of someone special to them. A number of things stand out about Tabitha. First, because of the number of widows, her acts of generosity must have taken place over a long period of time. Second, as a skilled person, Tabitha had spent a lot of her time and money making the garments that the widows needed. The widows were obviously proud of the clothes that Tabitha had made for them. The clothes weren't quickly sown sacks that could be produced in a short period of time. Third, Tabitha gave her time, skills and money cheerfully. She was well liked and was sadly missed by everyone who knew her.

Tabitha's death left a 'hole' in the community. Everyone who knew her felt a great sense of loss and wondered how, if ever, anyone could fill her place. The community's sense of loss was so great that they sent two men to find Peter, who was in Lydda several miles away. What could the community hope for? Tabitha was already dead and the mourning process had begun. But the feeling of grief for Tabitha made all the community want to do 'something', anything but just accept that she was gone. Peter went to Joppa straight away and, after praying for Tabitha, ordered her to 'get up'.

Try to imagine the feelings of all those who knew Tabitha when she walked down the stairs with Peter. The person whom the community thought was dead had been returned to them by God. Tabitha had made an impression on people in her lifetime (and an even bigger one after being raised from the dead!). The things she did had a positive effect on people and her very personality had a lasting impact on everyone who met her. Do you think the same will be said of us?

Why do people bother to help those in need? Ask the group to think of some reasons for helping others.

- Is it because people care?
- Is it because they hope that other people will see their 'good deeds'?

Write some of the group's responses onto a flipchart. Finally, ask the group whether it matters about the reasons as long as somebody does something for the people who need help.

(Allow 5 minutes.)

Ask them to think of someone they know who is in need of some help or encouragement. Give each group member a candle to represent that person. Place a table in the middle of the room and suggest that each member of the group light their candle and put it on the table. Ask the group to be quiet and as each flame burns read the following:

Lord,
  it's a good thing
  that we have no idea,
  know absolutely zilch,
  haven't the faintest hope
  of being able to predict
  when we will finally wave goodbye
  to the human race.
But as I take each breath
  (which better not be my last!)
  I want to say
  thanks for my life to date,
  and as each day passes
  may there be many, many more of them.
Although life may have
  its ups and downs,
  I would prefer
  more of the ups and less of the downs.
And that goes for those people
  who may be inclined to think
  that their life is going downhill
  big time.
Give me the courage, Lord,
  to make a difference,
  to give a helping hand
  whenever it's needed,
  even at those times
  when it feels as if
  I'm sitting in a pit
  waiting for a rain cloud
  to take its juice somewhere else.
Help me, help us,
  to be the difference
  between a smile and a frown.

TODAY'S SPECIAL

Every shape, size, colour and hue

Acts 11:1-18: Peter reports to the Church in Jerusalem

Equipment:
several tubes of Smarties (or similar coloured sweets)
dice
music and lyrics or drama sketch

Distribute the Smarties (or coloured sweets) randomly amongst the group. It doesn't matter if some of the group appear to have a few more sweets than others, it might add to the fun. Allocate a colour to each number of the dice, e.g. 1=red, 2=yellow and so on. There may be more than six colours but, again, that doesn't matter as long as you only allocate six numbers to six colours.

In turn, each member of the group rolls the dice and eats the sweet corresponding to the number they roll. If they haven't got the colour sweet that corresponds to the dice then they cannot eat any sweet. If a group member throws a 'six' on the dice, they can choose whether to eat the sweet relating to that number or try to swap one of their sweets with another group member for another colour. Continue rolling the dice in turn. Eventually, some of the group will have eaten all of their sweets, some will have colours which are not represented on the dice and some cannot roll the right number to finish eating their sweets.

(Allow 10 minutes for this activity.)

It's surprising how quickly and easily we can become either prejudiced or intolerant. Take a look at 'As I come to you' by Mick Dalton (*World Wide Worship No. 1*) or 'Let there be love' by Dave Bilbrough (*The source*, 317). Alternatively, you might like to use the drama sketch *The Wrinklies get sweet* (see page 111).

(Allow approximately 5 minutes.)

Ask the group how they felt during the sweet game.

- How quickly did they start to lose interest in certain coloured sweets?
- Did they try to 'swap' sweets for those that they favoured more?
- What point was the game trying to 'get across'?

Read Acts 11:1-18.

Peter, once one of many fishermen to work along the shores of Lake Galilee, had come a long way since being called by Jesus to become a disciple. At first hand Peter had experienced the miracles and the heartache of Jesus' ministry. He'd followed, questioned and rejected Jesus but now had become a respected leader of the Christians in and around Jerusalem.

The message of Jesus had affected many people and many more were becoming followers of Jesus. The widespread 'Gospel' was attracting both Jews and non-Jews (Gentiles). This was beginning to cause a problem amongst those Jews who believed that the Gospel of Jesus was only for Jews. Peter had already been faced with this issue and was certain that God treated everyone the same (see Acts 10:34-36). Now the issue was becoming contentious, arguments and dissension threatened to cause a split within the Church.

Many of the people who had accepted God's message wanted the Gentiles to become just like them: Jews. This meant adopting the Jewish way of life and traditions, rejecting their identity and exchanging it for another. The bottom line was that the Jewish believers didn't feel they could accept the Gentiles for who they were.

Peter had to step in and relate what had happened in the town of Joppa, where God had insisted that prejudice and racial discrimination had no part in God's plans. Once the people heard what God had said and that the Holy Spirit made no distinction between Jew and Gentile, then the arguments stopped and everyone began to worship God.

Accepting people for what they are is never easy, particularly when someone behaves very differently from us. God looks on each one of us as equals. He loves us for who we are and not what we may become. If God accepts everyone, irrespective of history, tradition, behaviour or appearance, then perhaps we should do the same.

As a group, try to define the word 'prejudice'.

- Are we prejudiced at times without realising it?
- What about in sport?
- How do we feel when we see images of people suffering because of starvation, war, intolerance or hatred?
- Is anyone to blame for people being homeless?
- Are there other instances where prejudice is apparent?
- How do we react?

- Do we feel uncomfortable with people of another race, belief, tradition or lifestyle?
- How easy/difficult is it to see things from God's perspective?

(Allow 5 minutes.)

Ask the group to be quiet for a few moments while you read the following:

Lord,
    I can appreciate the colours
    in a field full of flowers.
I can smell the richness
    of the differing scents
    as the breeze blows across every plant.
I can hear an orchestra
    of sounds in the air,
    with each whisper of life
    giving an identity,
    a unique expression
    of living
    in a world of variety.
I appreciate the difference
    in everything that surrounds me.
Each building, tree, flower or person
    combines to make
    a tapestry of existence.
Lord,
    thank you for being
    the creator of all things,
    the giver of life
    and a Father to humanity
    in a world of variety.

THE WRINKLIES GET SWEET

Characters Old 1 and Old 2, who find that there's more to a packet of sweets than simply taste.

Scene The aged grumps are sitting on a wall watching everything and everybody pass by. Wearing the loudest T-shirts that can be found at a jumble sale, the grumps are enjoying chewing sweets and commenting on whatever takes their fancy.

Props two bags of sweets
walking sticks
gaudy T-shirts

Old 2 *(Sucking busily on chewy sweet)* Hmmm, rather nice.

Old 1 *(Looks to the right and the left)* Where, did I blink?

Old 2 *(Still sucking sweet)* Very tasty.

Old 1 *(Getting agitated)* Where?

Old 2 What do you mean 'where'? What are you on about?

Old 1 What are *you* on about?

Old 2 *(Licks lips)* Creamy toffee.

Old 1 *(Taps side of head)* Reckon you're a few sweet wrappers short of a bag, myself.

Old 2 I wouldn't expect you to understand the finer things in life.

Old 1 *(Sniffs)* I know what I like and I like what I know.

Old 2 Precisely.

Old 1 And what's that supposed to mean?

Old 2 Well, come on. Who was it that found a half-chewed toffee in his coat pocket and then stuffed it straight into his mouth?

Old 1 I picked the fluff off first.

Old 2 And you call that being refined?

Old 1 Better than spitting the fluff out.

Old 2 I can't think of a more gruesome sight.

Old 1 I can.

Old 2 If you're referring to the time that you sneezed and your false teeth flew out of the window and hit old man Grub on the back of the head, don't mention it.

Old 1 *(Shows teeth and clicks together)* OK.

Old 2 You've got some disgusting habits.

Old 1 *(Snootily)* Refined and perfected over the years. *(Points with walking stick)* Bet you two toffees to a marshmallow that bloke doesn't get that sack of flour onto that cart.

Old 2 Right, you're on.

(Both grumps stare in front of them.)

Old 1 Oooh, he's about to drop it.

Old 2 Hang on, wait a minute. Here he goes, up, up and *(strikes the air with his fist)* YES, he does it. Two toffees, please.

(Old 1 hands over two toffees grudgingly.)

Old 2 Thank you.

Old 1 It was a fix.

Old 2 You what? You're just a poor loser.

Old 1 No, I'm not, then. The bloke tried too hard. Typical of some of these foreigners. Give them somewhere to live, a job and access to some of our finest markets and they take advantage of you. Can't trust them.

Old 2 Just because you lost a bet you blame everyone who looks different to you.

Old 1 No, I don't, then. Making a point, that's what.

Old 2 Making a fool of yourself, more like.

Old 1 And I suppose you think it's OK to have all these foreigners around?

Old 2 Live and let live I say.

Old 1 You would. You won the bet.

Old 2 Nothing to do with it. Here, *(offers bag of mixed sweets)* take one.

Old 1 Ta, don't mind if I do. *(Puts hand in bag and pulls out a sweet)*

Old 2 Do you like that sweet?

Old 1 I'll like it a whole lot better when it's in my mouth.

Old 2 *(Offers bag of sweets again)* Have another.

Old 1 Have you forgotten to take your tablets today?

Old 2 No, take them as regular as clockwork.

Old 1 Best way. It's good to be regular. I go every . . .

Old 2 *(Interrupts quickly)* Just pick another sweet rather than go into your morning routine.

Old 1 *(Puts hand in bag and picks another sweet)* Ta.

Old 2 Do you like that sweet too?

Old 1 Course I do. Why shouldn't I?

Old 2 No reason. It's nice to have a selection to choose from, though.

Old 1 *(Sucking sweet)* Variety. A taste of something different.

Old 2 Just like life, then.

Old 1 You what?

Old 2 Life. A variety, a taste of something different, you said.

Old 1 I meant sweets!

Old 2 And life. It's like a garden, rich in colours, smells, sights and sounds.

Old 1 You're barking, you are. Bet you three toffees to two marshmallows that pigeon lands on Ma Smith's washing-line and does a . . .

Old 2 I know, they eat plenty of fruit. Keeps them regular. Make it four toffees and you've got a bet.

TODAY'S SPECIAL

No mere dream

Acts 16:9-15: Paul's vision in Troas

Equipment:
paper, pens and envelopes
flipchart
music and lyrics

Distribute the paper and pens to the group. Have prepared a list (on the flipchart) of ten dreams or ambitions that you would like to achieve during the next ten years. Show the group your list of ambitions and chat about what you might do to achieve them.

Ask each member of the group to make a list, on their pieces of paper, of ten dreams or ambitions that *they* would like to achieve over the next ten years, for example career, qualifications, hobby, or relationships. If some of the group feel able, ask them to share with the others one or two of their ambitions and how they would go about achieving them.

(Allow 10 minutes for this activity.)

We can have short-term and long-term dreams or ambitions, some of which may require little effort while others present a major challenge. Whichever it may be, none of our ambitions will just happen without each of us doing something about them. We have to behave like the tortoise: stick our necks out.

Take a look at 'Lord, you have my heart' by Martin Smith (*Re:source 2000*, 9) or 'Faithful One' by Brian Doerksen (*The source*, 89).

(Allow approximately 5 minutes.)

Everybody has at least one dream or ambition that rattles around their head and prods their consciousness at regular intervals.

Read Acts 16:9-15.

Paul and his friends had been extremely busy travelling all over the place telling people about the good news of Jesus. Just before they arrived in Troas they had expected to spend some time in Phrygia and Galatia (parts of Turkey). In some way the Holy Spirit told them not to preach there and to carry on towards Troas (north-west Turkey).

Having trusted the instructions of the Holy Spirit, Paul and his friends were now told (in a dream) to go to Macedonia (eastern Greece). Twice Paul and his companions had been guided by the Holy Spirit and twice they had trusted that what they had been told was right. When they arrived in Macedonia, things were not quite what they expected.

Usually, the first thing Paul did was to go to a synagogue and share the good news of Jesus with everyone who would listen. After a few days of wondering what they were doing in Macedonia, the group went in search of a synagogue so that they could do what they thought they had to do. They found a place by the river where some women were gathered. One woman, Lydia, whose name indicates that she may once have been a slave but was now a free woman, was already a worshipper of God and was eager to hear what Paul had to say. It is quite probable that Lydia was a Gentile (non-Jew) and Paul's willingness to talk with her was another indication of God's care for the individual, regardless of who or what they were.

Paul had to place his trust in God because, as a Jew, he really shouldn't have been talking to a Gentile. Second, Lydia presuaded him to accept an invitation to go to her home, which was breaking a Jewish taboo regarding hospitality from non-Jews, on top of which Paul was accepting the invitation from a single woman!

Paul desperately needed to trust that God had everything under control, and hang on to what he was preaching: 'Faith in Christ Jesus is what makes each of you equal with each other, whether you are a Jew or a Greek, a slave or a free person, a man or a woman' (Galatians 3:28).

Paul had to put his faith in God and be directed by the Holy Spirit, even though some situations were difficult and it meant ignoring tradition or social customs. Faith was something Paul had to live each day. It was never easy and all the evidence may have suggested to others that he was absolutely barking, but Paul's experience taught him that God loved him and that trust was a two-way relationship.

Ask the group what they thought about Paul's actions. Was he doing the right thing by listening to God? Should Paul have been a little bit more careful about where he went and what he did?

Refer to the list of ten dreams that the group wrote down earlier. Suggest that each of the group re-examines the list and underlines those dreams which they feel happy chatting to God about. Are there any dreams which they feel uneasy about underlining?

Ask the group to fold their lists and place them in an envelope. Seal the envelopes and write the date on the front. Either collect the envelopes and tell the group that you will put them in a secure place or ask each individual to put them somewhere secure. Decide upon a date when the whole group would feel happy about opening the envelopes (possibly six months or even a year later). Some of the questions to consider at that time will be:

- Have any of the dreams been achieved or do any of them need altering?
- Have they chatted to God about their dreams?
- What happened?

(Allow 5 minutes.)

Ask the group to be quiet for a few moments as you read the following:

Psalm 62:5-10.
Only God gives inward peace, and I depend on him.
God alone is the mighty rock that keeps me safe,
  and he is the fortress where I feel secure.
God saves me and honours me.
He is that mighty rock where I find safety.
Trust God, my friends,
  and always tell him each one of your concerns.
God is our place of safety.

We humans are only a breath;
  none of us are truly great.
All of us together weigh less than a puff of air.
Don't trust in violence or depend on dishonesty
  or rely on great wealth.

TODAY'S SPECIAL

Turnaround

Acts 16:16-34: Paul and Silas are put in jail

Equipment:
selection of envelopes and sheets of paper
paper and pens
a number of very small boxes
music and lyrics

As the group arrive greet them with an abrupt 'hello' and carry on looking at the sheets of paper (which should be covered with numbers and lots of writing). Mutter something about 'parasites', 'piranha fish', 'financial carnivores' and such like. After a short while apologise to the group and tell them that you are having problems trying to sort out all the demands for your hard-earned money. Suggest that you feel totally besieged by the constant deluge of letters through your door. Have the group any ideas how you can 'sort out' your problems?

Return the few coins that the group collected for you (!) and give each of them a piece of paper and a pen. Ask the group to write down problems which they have experienced or are currently experiencing. When they have finished, ask them to fold the paper in half and keep it safe until later.

Ask the group how they feel when 'problems' occur which cause them to worry or become afraid of the future.

(Allow 10 minutes for this activity.)

What may be a problem to some people is a minor irritation to others. Take a look at 'There is a light that shines on us' by Howard Williams (*Re:source 2000*, 13) or 'You love me as you found me' by Russell Fragar (*The source*, 602).

(Allow approximately 5 minutes.)

It's impossible to avoid the negative feelings that problems cause. How we deal with our feelings and the problems is what really matters.

Read Acts 16:16-34.

Paul and Silas had experienced quite a lot of hostility and hassle on their journeys and quite possibly thought that they could deal with most things that came their way. After a brief confrontation with a slave girl and an evil spirit, Paul and Silas found themselves on the wrong side of the law.

They were attacked, stripped, beaten with a whip and thrown in jail. Once inside, the stench of rotting food, unwashed prisoners and lack of toilet facilities would have made Paul and Silas, with their feet chained to heavy blocks of wood, feel a little uncomfortable! But, rather than become grumpy and complain about their accommodation, both Paul and Silas decided to pray and worship God.

At around midnight a strong earthquake wrecked the jail (was Paul and Silas' singing *that* bad?). All the prisoners suddenly found their hands and feet free of chains. Somehow Paul managed to persuade the other prisoners not to escape and was able to prevent the jailer from committing suicide (the prisoners were the jailer's responsibility).

At this point the situation was turned right around. The jailer, recognising that there was something more to Paul and Silas than cuts and bruises, knelt in front of them and asked them what he must do to know the living God. Most people in Paul and Silas' position would have asked for something to eat and drink, and possibly somewhere to bathe their wounds. But not Paul and Silas. The first thing they did was to tell everyone in the jailer's house about Jesus. Then they got their wounds bathed and were fed.

The next morning the order came for Paul and Silas to be freed. Things were looking up. Again, most of us would have been glad the whole mess was over and done, but not Paul and Silas. Revealing that they were Roman citizens, which gave them special rights and privileges, Paul and Silas stayed where they were until the officials came to the jail, apologised and escorted them out of jail.

One moment Paul and Silas are enjoying the smell of the blossom on the trees and the sun on their faces and the next they are given a good kicking and thrown in prison where the stench must have made their stomachs turn. Unable to move, they chat to God and thank him for their lives! As a result of their determination not to allow events to hang like a cloud over them, the jailer and his family find a faith in God which would never have happened if Paul and Silas had acted like most prisoners and moaned about their predicament. Are we able to see beyond the immediate problem and thank God for being God?

Remind the group about the pieces of paper on which they wrote about their problems earlier. Place the papers into one of the small boxes and put it in the middle of the floor. Arrange the other boxes to form a wall, with the first box at the base of the wall. Ask the group what they think this could represent. The idea is for the original box, containing the problems, to be seen as a sort of foundation, experiences that we can learn from and use as we 'build' our lives.

Take the sheets of paper out of the original box and place one sheet of paper in each of the other boxes and rebuild the wall. All of us experience problems. Some of us experience problems others haven't had to face. Together we can offer support and encouragement, having 'lived' the problem and dealt with its consequences.

(Allow 5 minutes.)

Ask the group to be quiet and consider how we can each encourage one another as we face different problems in our lives. While the group are quiet read the following:

Romans 8:28, 31-32.
We know that God is always at work for the good of everyone who loves him . . . What can we say about all this? If God is on our side, can anyone be against us? God did not keep back his only Son, but he gave him for us. If God did this, won't he freely give us everything else?

TODAY'S SPECIAL

What a noise!

Acts 2:1-21: The coming of the Holy Spirit

Equipment:
cards
paper and pens
music and lyrics

Once the group have arrived, give each of them a number (say, 1-10) and two cards, each with a different letter of the alphabet written on them. Call out three numbers, and ask the group members, who were given those numbers to get together. Call out another three numbers and so on until the group are in teams of three. The object of the exercise is for each team to use their letters to make as many words as possible in the time given. Allocate a scoring system which rewards longer words, e.g. two letters = 1 point, three letters = two points, four letters = three points and so on. The team with the highest score are declared the winners.

Being presented with random letters and a task to complete is always a challenge. What were some of the problems the teams encountered?

(Allow 10 minutes for this activity.)

When faced with a difficult or confusing situation, it is often easier to turn away or try and ignore the situation. Sometimes we don't have the luxury of choosing to opt out!

Take a look at 'The Spirit of the Lord' by Graham Kendrick (*Re:source 2000*, 15) or 'Down the mountain the river flows' by Andy Park (*The source*, 83).

(Allow approximately 5 minutes.)

What did the group think of the lyrics for the chosen song?

Read Acts 2:1-21.

The Feast of Pentecost was a time to celebrate a successful harvest. It was a time when all male Israelites would make a peace offering to God, asking for forgiveness, and would remember God's help in getting them out of captivity in Egypt. Jerusalem would have been bursting at the seams as people gathered to make their peace offering and celebrate

God's goodness. Many people would have travelled a long way to celebrate at the temple in Jerusalem. As a result, it would have been possible to hear many different languages in the streets (see verses 7-11).

At this same time God fulfilled a promise that Jesus had made and sent the Holy Spirit on the disciples as God's representative. To their amazement everyone within earshot of the disciples heard these men from Galilee talking in many different languages. The Holy Spirit had given each of the disciples the ability to express their feelings in a foreign language. This demonstration of the Holy Spirit had two purposes. First, it was a fulfilment of a promise and one which gave the followers of Jesus the ability to act with God as their authority. Second, it was a celebration. It was an expression of the disciples' heartfelt thanks for all that God had done and would do.

The use of so many different languages appeared to be God's way of saying that everything that Jesus had accomplished was now to be shared throughout the world; language was no barrier.

Peter, whose education was minimal, stood up in front of a huge crowd and explained what God was doing. The time had come for the disciples (now called apostles) to spread the good news of Jesus.

Give each member of the group a piece of paper and a pen. In Acts 2:12, the demonstration of the Holy Spirit had left everyone both excited and confused. There may be many things about God, Jesus and the Holy Spirit that are not altogether clear or need some explanation. Invite the group to write a question on the piece of paper about something which has been rattling around their head for a while. Ask the group to be honest and write down, no matter how basic the question might appear, whatever it is that they have trouble getting to grips with.

You may like to respond to some of the questions immediately or set aside a period of time each week to try and answer one question from the group. Make this time an honest, no-holds-barred session where anyone can feel totally comfortable to ask whatever is on their mind. You might like to have a special place on a notice board where group members can pin a question.

(Allow 5 minutes.)

PENTECOST: WHIT SUNDAY

30

Ask the group to be quiet for a few moments while you read the following prayer:

Lord,
  I really can't get my head around
  all this 'thee, thou and therefore' stuff.
It drives me round the bend and over the hill.
What does it all mean?
Is it some sort of code for the initiated?
A kind of secret language
  that only those in the know understand?
Do we need a translator or interpreter
  to explain what's going on
  and what we need to do?
Should there be a sort of 'idiots' guide'
  to help us say the 'right' things at the 'right' time? –
  so that we don't stand up when we should be sitting down.
Perhaps you could suggest
  that someone puts a few dictionaries
  next to the hymn books,
  although I really think
  that we'd never sing a word or a note.
We'd be too busy looking in the dictionary
  trying to find out
  what we were singing about,
  or what we were trying to say
  if only we knew what we'd said!
I think we need
  the Holy Spirit
  to descend on a few of the congregation
  and get them to speak
  in a language
  that we can all understand.
Until that time,
  you'll have to guess what I mean
  'cos the only word I've got sorted
  comes at the end of a line. Amen.

TODAY'S SPECIAL

Stones in our shoes

Romans 5:1-5: What it means to be acceptable to God

Equipment:
selection of squeaky toys
blindfolds
pebbles
music and lyrics

Mark out an area as large as your room/space allows. Place the squeaky toys randomly around the selected area. Ask three or four volunteers from the group to leave the room. While the volunteers are out of the room, ask another member of the group to 'rearrange' the toys (just in case one of the volunteers thinks they may have been clever and tried to memorise the position of the toys). Blindfold the first volunteer and bring them back into the room. Explain to the volunteer that their task is to walk from one end of the marked area to the other without stepping on any of the toys.

At this point insist that the rest of the group be quiet and not attempt to try and 'advise' the volunteer.

Once the volunteer has completed the task, count the number of 'squeaks', if any, that they made during their attempt. Invite the next blindfolded volunteer into the room and repeat the task. The person who completes the task with the fewest 'squeaks' is awarded a squeaky toy as a reminder of their 'squeakless' ability.

(Allow 10 minutes for this activity.)

Trying to avoid putting your foot where you don't want to tread is often really difficult.

Have a look at 'You rescued me' by Geoff Bullock (*The source*, 605) or 'To be in your presence' by Noel Richards (*The source*, 524).

(Allow approximately 5 minutes.)

Whether we like it or not, we will come up against situations which threaten our confidence and make it feel as if we're walking on thin ice.

Read Romans 5:1-5.

You know how embarrassing it is. You've walked for what seems like miles with a huge boulder fighting for space in your shoe. The boulder prods and jabs at every opportunity as it attempts to evict your foot from its previously comfy surroundings. You stop, take off your shoe to reveal to the world the size of this enormous piece of granite . . . a tiny speck on the end of your finger. The embarrassment, the groans and insults that everyone throws at you for complaining about a speck of dust. But they don't understand. To you, the piece of grit felt like a considerable portion of a mountain. You were just about to phone whichever government organisation deals with the height of mountains and inform them that one of their mountains isn't where it should be . . . it's where you don't want it to be.

Other people might think your complaints unjustified but for you the pain was genuine. The discomfort was all too real. Nothing else felt as important as putting the mountain back where it belonged and recapturing that feeling of comfort.

At times, it feels as if our lives are plagued by irritating little bits of grit that are intent on annoying us at every opportunity. Sometimes it's not bits of grit that cause us discomfort, it's huge rocks that have placed themselves just where we want to walk! We have a choice. We can stop and remove the grit or carry on walking! No contest! At other times it's not so simple. We cannot always remove or avoid the rocks in our path, we need to learn how to climb over them.

Of course, we always have the option of either stopping where we are or turning around and going back the way we came. But God encourages us to go forward and face the rocks, learn how to deal with them.

For some, the 'rocks' may be relationships or financial difficulties. For other people it might be their career or education that is causing them to feel as if their progress has ground to a halt. We can be certain of one fact: we will never learn how to deal with those obstacles if we turn our backs on them. Dealing with the 'rocks' takes courage, it often involves pain, frustration and anger. It is at these times that God longs for us to ask him for help, to get him involved and longs to teach us how to climb. It's never easy but it makes for an interesting journey.

Give each member of the group a pebble. Ask them to think about a situation in their life that is giving them pain. Suggest that they ask God to get involved and help them deal with the situation. If they want God to get involved, ask them to place the pebble on the floor in the middle of the room.

Offer to chat with any of the group if they feel that it would help to discuss the situation.

(Allow 5 minutes.)

Once those members who want to have placed their pebble on the floor, ask them all to be quiet while you read the following:

From Psalm 91.
Live under the protection of God Most High
  and stay in the shadow of God All-Powerful . . .
The Lord Most High is your fortress.
Run to him for safety,
  and no terrible disasters will strike you or your home.
God will command angels to protect you
  wherever you go.
They will carry you in their arms,
  and you won't hurt your feet on the stones . . .
The Lord says,
  'If you love me and truly know who I am,
  I will rescue you and keep you safe.
  When you are in trouble, call out to me.
  I will answer and be there to protect and honour you.
  You will live a long life and see my saving power.'

UNIT 32

32

TODAY'S SPECIAL

Sorry, could you repeat that?

Galatians 1:1-12: The only true message

Equipment:
cards or paper, and pens
music and lyrics or drama sketch

Explain to the group that you would like to start today's session with a reading from the Bible.

You will need to have prepared some paper or cards which contain the following Bible reading *but* with the underlined words omitted. The missing words are to be filled in by the group later in the session.

Love.

What if I could speak all languages of humans and of angels?

If I did not love others, I would be nothing more than a noisy gong or a clanging cymbal.

What if I could prophesy and understand all secrets and all knowledge? And what if I had faith that moved mountains?

I would be nothing, unless I loved others. What if I gave away all that I owned and let myself be burnt alive? I would gain nothing, unless I loved others.

Love is patient, never jealous, boastful, proud or rude.

Love isn't selfish or quick-tempered.

It doesn't keep a record of wrongs that others do. Love rejoices in the truth, but not in evil.

Love is always supportive, loyal, hopeful and trusting.

Love never fails!

1 Corinthians 13:1-8.

You might like to read the Bible verses again, slowly, emphasising the underlined words.

(Allow 10 minutes for this activity.)

In the Bible reading, verse 6 states that 'Love rejoices in the truth'. How do we know when we hear the truth? Can we be easily deceived by half-truths and suggestions?

Take a look at 'Jesus, restore to us again' by Graham Kendrick (*The source*, 295) or 'Thank you for saving me' by Martin Smith (*The source*, 472). Alternatively, you might like to use the drama sketch *The Wrinklies lose the plot* (see page 130).

(Allow approximately 5 minutes.)

We are bombarded with words almost every second of the day. Everywhere we look we see words used to persuade us to buy and collect, or save for certain products. How can we determine which, if any, of the advertisers are being honest?

Read Galatians 1:1-12.

Galatia was a large Roman province which occupied parts of central Turkey. Many Galatians had become believers of the Gospel of Jesus Christ but had recently been subjected to the 'extra' beliefs of a group of religious people. These religious people were known as the 'Judaizers', a group who firmly believed that to follow Christ also meant becoming Jews, or following the Jewish tradition. The Judaizers believed that Gentiles (non-Jews), had to become Jews before they could really consider themselves 'Christians' and followers of the true God. It was this insistence by the Judaizers on performing rituals and adopting traditions that so angered Paul.

Paul considered that the very foundation of the Christian message was a new life (salvation) which was God's gift to everyone who believed in him and the Gospel of Jesus Christ. To claim that God would have nothing to do with you if you didn't try and earn his love was destructive and made the sacrifice of Jesus (his death and resurrection) almost meaningless.

Paul stressed that the Galatians, by being persuaded to adopt Jewish traditions, were listening to another message, one different from that which Paul had given, which itself was not made up or a collection of folk tales, but was a message direct from Jesus.

Paul felt it was vital that the Galatian believers were not deceived into thinking that they had to earn God's love. There never was and still isn't any merit system that could 'buy' what God freely gave.

No one is perfect, and nor can we be. Thinking that we must do the 'right' things and say the 'right' things is totally missing the point of what Jesus had to say and do. There are always people who would have us believe that we must behave in a certain way before God will have anything to do with us. The truth is that God loves us and that love is freely given, not earned or the result of reaching a required number of merits. Anything that teaches anything different isn't the truth, and that really *is* Good News!

Give every member of the group your pre-prepared cards, or sheets of paper which have the Bible verses written on them but with the underlined words omitted (see 'Nibbles'). Ask everyone, individually, to try and fill in the blanks, putting in the words which they think are correct.

When they have completed this, ask if anyone would like to read their completed verses. Were they correct? Do any other members of the group think that some of the words are wrong? Listen to a couple of other 'completed' verses and then present the group with the correct Bible reading from 1 Corinthians 13:1-8.

- How difficult did the group find this task?
- Why was it hard to put in the correct words?
- How can we know if the words are wrong?

(Allow 5 minutes.)

Ask the group to think about what 'truth' really means. Being truthful and honest is never the easiest of things to do. It often takes a lot of courage. While the group are thinking, read the following prayer:

Lord,
   getting confused
   seems to be an occupational hazard
   of living.
Everyone has an opinion
   and everyone insists they're right!
Words seem to surround me
   like a dust cloud on a hot day.
They blur my vision and dull my senses.
I'm not sure which way to turn.
Do this, do that,
   don't do this, don't do that.
What am I supposed to do?
I need to be able
   to pick out the truth
   from a pile of garbage.
I need to see the truth
   stand out like a neon light
   on a dark night.
Help me, Lord,
   to know you,
   to see, hear and know the truth
   in a land of confusion.

THE WRINKLIES LOSE THE PLOT

Characters	Two aged grumps who can't seem to agree on anything, even when it's as plain as a packet of ready-salted crisps that they shouldn't believe everything they hear.
Scene	The two grumps are seated on a bench. The day hasn't started well for either of them and things are going down-hill fast.
Props	bench two baggy jumpers with gaudy designs two hats pair of walking sticks

Old 1 *(Sniffs)*

Old 2 *(Coughs)*

Old 1 *(Sniffs again and leans on walking stick)*

Old 2 *(Coughs again and prods ground with walking stick)*

Old 1 *(Sniffs)* Should see a vet.

Old 2 Did you sniff?

Old 1 I wouldn't leave it too long if I were you. Might turn into something nasty . . . *(mumbles)* with any luck.

Old 2 Did you mumble something or have your intestines finally given up on the unequal challenge of dealing with everything you shovel into your mouth?

Old 1 Oooh! Who's got out of bed the wrong side then?

Old 2 At least I slept in a bed. More than can be said for some I could mention.

Old 1 *(Angrily)* And what's that supposed to mean?

Old 2 Just something I heard in passing.

Old 1 Have you been listening to vicious gossip?

Old 2 *(With mock surprise)* What, me listen to gossip? Never!

Old 1 Don't give me all that rubbish. You're the reason the local paper had to shut down. Nobody bought a copy of the paper when they could hear all the news from you for free.

Old 2 Hey! There's nothing wrong in passing the time of day with your neighbours.

Old 1 Didn't say there was. But people got a little suspicious when you rattled that collection box under their nose every time they stopped for a chat.

Old 2 It was all for charity.

Old 1 Really?

Old 2 An extremely good cause. One very close to my heart.

Old 1 And what would that be?

Old 2 Prevention Of Tired Toes Yawning.

Old 1 What?

Old 2 POTTY for short.

Old 1 You're telling me. Are there lots of members?

Old 2 Not yet.

Old 1 A national organisation?

Old 2 Not quite. One day perhaps, but until then . . .

Old 1 *(Interrupts)* Let me guess, you're the only member?

Old 2 Correct.

Old 1 You've got a nerve.

Old 2 You have to look after yourself these days, nobody else will.

Old 1 *(Rearranges hat on head)* True. Mind you, there's plenty of people who are only *too* willing when it comes to interfering in your life.

Old 2 Now, that's definitely true.

Old 1 Sometimes I wonder what they'd do with their days if they didn't spend them gossiping and spreading vicious rumours.

Old 2 Gossip runs through their veins, it's their life-blood. Deprive them of scandal and they'd shrivel-up and die.

Old 1 *(Taps walking stick on the ground)* Very true.

Old 2 That's one word they don't know the meaning of.

Old 1 What, 'true'?

Old 2 Exactly.

Old 1 So there's nothing behind the rumour I heard yesterday?

Old 2 *(Acts agitated)* What rumour, who, when, where?

Old 1 Aren't you over-reacting?

Old 2 Not a bit. Particularly when some of those rumour-mongers are like piranha fish; shred a person's character to ribbons they can.

Old 1 You claim it's not true then?

Old 2 How can I? I haven't a clue what you're on about.

Old 1	So, you flatly deny it?
Old 2	No, er, yes, erm, I would if I knew what you were referring to.
Old 1	Aren't you protesting a bit too much?
Old 2	Of course I am. I don't need unnecessary gossip at my age.
Old 1	Dangerous.
Old 2	It would be if her indoors heard about it.
Old 1	About what?
Old 2	I've absolutely no idea.
Old 1	Neither have I. Still, *(rearranges hat)* you can always rely on a hat.
Old 2	*(Adjusts own hat)* Every time.

TODAY'S SPECIAL

What a change!

Galatians 1:11-24: How Paul became an apostle

Equipment:
paper and pens
music and lyrics

Give each member of the group a piece of paper and a pen. Ask them to write at the top of the page: 'I wish I were/weren't . . .'

Chat about some of the things that you would like to change, either about yourself or about situations that annoy or worry you. Then ask the group to complete the sentence by writing two or three things that they would either change about themselves or situations they would like to alter in some way.

(Allow 10 minutes for this activity.)

We all feel that there are things about ourselves that we'd like to change or alter. Sometimes the things we'd like to change can become really difficult for us to deal with or cause us distress.

Have a look at 'Seasons may change' by Matt Redman (*The source new songs*, 56) or 'Here I am once again' by Craig Musseau (*The source new songs*, 15).

(Allow approximately 5 minutes.)

Once we begin to think about change, it's almost impossible to be satisfied with leaving things the way they were.

Read Galatians 1:11-24.

Some cynics would argue that nothing really changes, everything remains the same. Any perceived changes are cosmetic and underneath nothing is any different.

Paul, in writing to the Church in Galatia, wanted the Christians there to understand that he *was* a changed man. Previously, he'd been fully committed to getting rid of the Church and giving every Christian a chance to meet their maker . . . prematurely. Paul had also been devoted to the tradition of the Pharisees, where an extensive set of rules and regulations had been passed from generation to generation by word of mouth.

Paul was a man who, by reputation, was known to be against everything that Jesus had said and done. Not only was he totally opposed to Jesus and his followers, he actively set about destroying everything that had any connection with this 'new' Gospel.

At the time of Paul's writing, he'd changed. He'd turned around and instead of being against Jesus, he was now actively preaching the message that he once tried to destroy. It must have been very difficult for anyone who knew about Paul to believe the changes were for real.

In his letter, Paul stresses that he didn't spend time being instructed in a new belief system or listening to a different set of rules and regulations. In fact, Paul went out of his way (to Arabia) so that he wasn't influenced by any other teaching or ideas.

To some people, especially the Pharisees and religious leaders, the change in Paul was a scandal. He was a disgrace to Judaism. Paul acknowledged what he had once been and emphasised what he had now become. To him it was no disgrace, God had changed his life and things would never be the same again. At times, Paul may have wondered why the changes caused so much antagonism and hatred. But he never regretted what God had done, even though he suffered as a direct result of the changes that God had brought about in his life.

There may be one or many things that we would like to see changed in our lives. Some of the things may be superficial while others may be rooted deep in our emotions. Whatever it is, God wants to get involved. He wants to be in at the beginning and be with us every step of the way. He hasn't said it will be a piece of cake and everything will be 'easy peasy'. But he has promised to be in it with us. Now that's reassuring.

Ask the group to look again at the things they'd like to change. Does anyone feel confident enough to chat with the group about what they'd like to change? This may be really difficult for some of the group, so don't push the issue. Rather, look at some of the more 'usual' things that people would like to change, for instance: being shy, insecure, too chatty; their physical appearance, lack of money, lifestyle, house, car, qualifications, success or lack of it.

- Why do we want to change these things?
- Is it wrong to want to change the way we look?

Be sensitive to the reasons given for wanting change. The last thing that most people want to hear is 'don't worry', or 'it'll sort itself out later'. Perhaps you could make some badges with the words: 'Fragile human being inside'.

(Allow 5 minutes.)

Suggest that the group spend a few moments in quiet while you read the following:

From Psalm 25.
I offer you my heart, Lord God, and I trust you.
Don't make me ashamed or let my enemies defeat me . . .
Show me your paths and teach me to follow;
guide me by your truth and instruct me.
You keep me safe, and I always trust you . . .
You lead humble people to do what is right
and to stay on your path.
In everything you do, you are kind and faithful
to everyone who keeps our agreement with you . . .
I always look to you,
because you rescue me from every trap.
I am lonely and troubled.
Show that you care and have pity on me.
My awful worries keep growing.
Rescue me from sadness.
See my troubles and misery and forgive my sins . . .
I come to you for shelter. Protect me, keep me safe,
and don't disappoint me.
I obey you with all my heart,
and I trust you, knowing that you will save me.'

TODAY'S SPECIAL

Rules, regulations and rigid hearts

Galatians 2:(11-14) 15-21: Paul corrects Peter at Antioch

Equipment:
pieces of card with instructions on
three pieces of card: one black, one white and one grey
music and lyrics

Prepare the cards so that each piece contains one of the followings instructions:

Turn left	Turn right
Turn around	Stop
Move two paces	Move four paces
Balance on one leg	Close your eyes
Move forward	Move backwards
Say 'quack'	Put your fingers in your ears
Ignore the next command	Repeat the previous command
Move one pace to the left	Move one pace to the right

Shuffle the cards. Select at least four 'victims' and stand them at different locations in the room. Ask one of the group to choose three cards and 'victim' number one carries out the written instructions. Return the cards to the pack, shuffle and ask another member of the group to choose three cards for 'victim' number two. Repeat the process as often as you wish. To make the game more 'active', prepare a set of cards for each 'victim' and have other members of the group read the instructions at the same time. This will result in all the 'victims' following the commands at the same time! Should be fun.

(Allow 10 minutes for this activity.)

Following instructions isn't always funny. At times it can cause us to feel constrained and trapped. Take a look at 'How do I know you love me?' by Mark Altrogge (*The source new songs*, 19) or 'Lord, my heart before you' by Trish Morgan (*The source new songs*, 40).

(Allow approximately 5 minutes.)

Being told what to do and when to do it is difficult. Admitting that someone else may be right may seem even harder. Whatever we think, being told the truth is hardly easy to accept, or should that be: 'easily hard to accept'?

Read Galatians 2:(11-14) 15-21.

Every day of the week we live according to rules and regulations. Some of these rules and regulations are formal, written laws that have consequences if we ignore them. At other times, the rules and regulations may be a result of the way we have been brought up by our parents and family, ways of behaving that reflect our childhood.

Very occasionally we react to situations in an unexpected, spontaneous way which other people may consider 'out of character'. Our friends, work mates or teachers may not have been exposed to such an instance of our behaviour but, at some time or other, we have acted or wanted to act in a way that confounds and surprises people.

Sometimes we may feel inhibited, unable to express ourselves in the way that we want to. We are afraid of what our peers may say should we refuse to conform to the 'expected' behaviour of the group.

Nobody likes to accept that their behaviour is a result of many social and political attitudes which 'shape' the way they behave.

In his letter to the Galatians, Paul is telling Peter that he cannot claim to have complete faith in Jesus Christ if he 'moulds' his behaviour to suit a particular group of people. Other people may accept us because of the way we conform to certain patterns of behaviour but is that a true reflection of who we are? The most important thing is to accept that God loves us *because* of the way we are. We cannot earn his love or generate a list of 'good deeds' that we can exchange for God's love. By putting our faith in Jesus Christ we have no need to make 'acceptance by other people' our number one priority. We don't need to conform to a list of rules and regulations that claims we are only acceptable to God if we behave in a certain way. As Paul says, if we could find acceptance by God through obeying a set of rules and regulations, what was the point of Christ dying? (verse 21). Make God your focus and accept the way *he* behaves. That's liberating!

Ask those members of the group, who were the 'victims' in the game played at the beginning of the session, how they felt about being 'directed' by someone else.

- Did they feel that some of the instructions weren't very helpful?
- Did they have a conflict in their own minds between what they were being told to do and what they wanted to do?
- Did they feel frustrated, annoyed or even angry regarding some of the commands?
- What did some of the other group members feel? Could they see that some of the instructions were taking the 'victim' the wrong way? Did they want to intervene?
- Can the group relate the feelings expressed through the game to any events in their own lives?
- Do they have any experience of feeling a conflict between what they want to do and what someone else wants them to do?
- Does advice or direction from another person create a conflict in their own minds between what they think is the right thing to do and what the other person thinks is the right thing to do?
- How can we resolve the issue?

(Allow 5 minutes.)

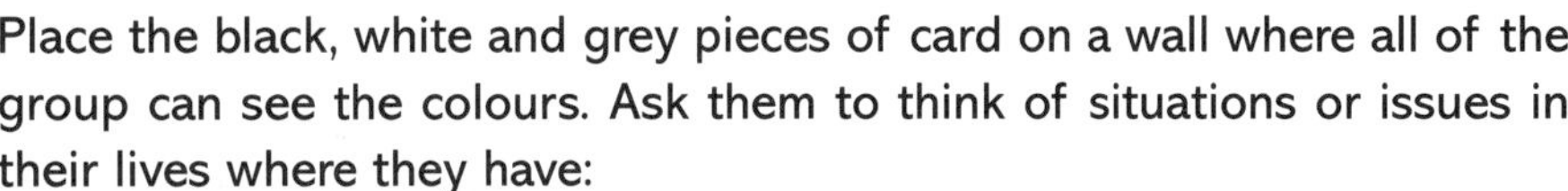

Place the black, white and grey pieces of card on a wall where all of the group can see the colours. Ask them to think of situations or issues in their lives where they have:

- accepted some advice or thought and prayed about the issue, and it has been resolved in the way they had hoped (white card)
- ignored advice and refused to listen to what they feel is the right thing to do, and the situation has turned sour (black card)
- listened to advice, thought and prayed, and still the issue or situation remains unresolved (grey card).

While the group are quiet, read the following:

Proverbs 3:5-6.
With all your heart you must trust the Lord
  and not in your own judgement.
Always let him lead you,
  and he will clear the road for you to follow.

TODAY'S SPECIAL

Does this still fit me?

Galatians 3:23-29: Slaves and children

Equipment:
bags of assorted children's clothes
cards, each of a different colour
candle
music and lyrics

Arrange the clothes into various bags. Make sure that most of the clothes are far too small for any member of the group. As the group arrive allocate each one a colour (red, blue, white, yellow, etc.). Depending on the number in your group, there should be some group members allocated the same colour.

Take the set of coloured cards, shuffle them, turn them so that the colours are face down and then ask one of the group to pick a card. Show the card to the group and every member who has been allocated that colour must, without looking, take an item of clothing from the bag and put it on.

Continue picking colour cards and getting the chosen group members to put on whatever item of clothing they pick out of the bag. After a while you should have every member of the group dressed in an assortment of ill-fitting clothes!

It might be fun to make the group continue to wear the clothing throughout the whole session!

(Allow 10 minutes for this activity.)

Feelings of discomfort and thinking that everyone looks a touch silly are quite normal when we try to wear items that we have clearly outgrown!

Take a look at 'Jesus, you're all I need' by Darlene Zschech (*The source new songs*, 31) or 'When the cares of life come' by Steve and Vikki Cook (*The source new songs*, 78).

(Allow approximately 5 minutes.)

Putting on clothes that we know are too small may seem daft but it's surprising how often, as Christians, we behave as if we have never grown up!

Read Galatians 3:23-29.
Paul's letter is not to any single Church in Galatia but to a number of Churches in that region. He is concerned that quite a few Christians are still trying to please God by conforming to a set of rules, or law.

To begin with, Paul attempts to put the record straight. He tells the Galatians that God knows only too well that following a law would prove difficult to do all the time. Although God made a covenant (a sort of contract) with Abraham, it was only intended to be the start of the journey which reached its destination with the arrival of Jesus Christ.

In the time of the Romans a certain slave (known as *paidagogos*) would have the responsibility for supervising and correcting the children of the family. When the children grew older, they had learned how to behave and now dealt directly with their father and were responsible to him for their actions.

This is the idea that Paul was trying to get across to the Churches in Galatia. The law could act as a guide but it was only a start, a sort of teacher, which could go just so far in preparing anyone for a relationship with God the Father. Paul emphasised that it was only faith in Jesus Christ which made a person acceptable to God. To say 'I have faith in Jesus Christ' and then continue to live according to the law was the same as a Roman person, having grown up and being told they were now free to develop a relationship with their father, ignoring that freedom and going back to the slave for guidance.

We have a similar choice to make. In the same way that we wouldn't buy clothes that were intended for someone a lot younger than ourselves, neither should we say we want a relationship with God the Father and then ignore the freedom that we have through Jesus Christ to chat with God and ask for his help. If we try to live our lives by superstition, performing elaborate rituals or attempting to earn God's favour, are we ignoring what Jesus Christ has done for us?

Just as we no longer make animal sacrifices, as was required under the law, nor are we expected to perform a complex ritual to get God's attention. Christ's sacrifice meant that we can have a relationship with God, anywhere, anytime. Perhaps it's time to experience some of that freedom which faith in Jesus Christ brings?

If the group are still wearing the children's clothes, it may be time to take them off and put them back into the bags.

Place the bags of clothes in the centre of the room. Ask the group how they felt wearing those clothes.

- What normally happens to clothes that are too small for us?
- Do we still shop in the same stores that our parents used to buy our baby clothes from?
- Why?

(Allow 5 minutes.)

Show the group a copy of the highway code. Select some of the road signs and ask if any of the group can identify the sign and explain what it means. Most of us who drive are familiar with many of the signs although hardly anybody can say they know what every sign means. If we tried to live by the highway code, we'd be stopping the car every few miles to refer to the book to find out what the sign meant. Most people who drive a car hardly ever refer to the highway code (perhaps some people need to!); they use their experience to get around safely. Although they know what most of the signs mean, they recognise that they are only a guide. To drive safely takes more than simply knowing what the signs mean.

Having faith in Jesus Christ needs more than a reliance on the Bible. The Bible is an important document which helps us to understand what God did and how other people related to God, but it's a guide. A relationship with God is a living experience, one to be shared daily.

Light a candle and place it where all the group can see it. Read the following:

John 8:12-19.
Once again Jesus spoke to the people. This time he said, 'I am the light of the world! Follow me, and you won't be walking in the dark. You will have the light that gives life.'

The Pharisees objected, 'You are only speaking for yourself, and what you say isn't true!'

Jesus replied: 'Even if I do speak for myself, what I say is true! I know where I came from and where I am going. But you don't know where I am from or where I am going. You judge in the same way that everyone else does, but I don't judge anyone. If I did judge, I would judge fairly, because I would not be doing it alone. The Father who sent me is here with me. Your law requires two witnesses to prove that something is true. I am one of my witnesses, and the Father who sent me is the other one.'

'Where is your Father?' they asked.

'You don't know me or my Father!' Jesus answered. 'If you knew me, you would know my Father.'

TODAY'S SPECIAL

Right, OK, er, well, you see . . .

Galatians 5:1, 13-25: Christ gives freedom

Equipment:
postcards
paper and pens
small wastepaper bin
music and lyrics

Write one of the following words on each of the postcards:

Anger	Love	Jealousy	Happiness
Patience	Selfishness	Faithfulness	Kindness
Envy	Peacefulness	Troublemaker	

Give each member of the group a number, up to the number of postcards used. Choose a number and let the corresponding group member pick one of the cards at random. The group member has ten seconds to look at the card and then must speak for thirty seconds about the subject on the card. They are allowed to use a story, incident or something they've seen in a film or TV programme to try and describe what the word means. They are not allowed to use any delaying tactics or pause during their thirty seconds. If someone pauses or runs out of words then that person is out of the game. Continue playing until all the cards are used up or there is a clear winner.

(Allow 10 minutes for this activity.)

We are affected by many of the words used in the previous section, but trying to explain what they mean to us can be an uncomfortable experience.

Take a look at 'Here I am, in that old place again' by Stuart Garrard and Martin Smith (*The source new songs*, 14) or 'I will come to you' by Reuben Morgan (*The source new songs*, 27).

(Allow approximately 5 minutes.)

How difficult did the group find describing the words used during the game? Were some words easier to explain than others? Why was that?

Read Galatians 5:1, 13-25.

The way we behave has a major impact not only on ourselves but on our family, friends and workmates. Paul starts this section of his letter to the Churches in Galatia with the statement, 'Christ has set us free!' (verse 1). But he then goes to great lengths to say that this freedom doesn't give us the liberty to do anything we want. In an odd turn of events, Paul suggests that by allowing ourselves to 'do what we want', we often resort to forms of behaviour that are far from healthy for all concerned. The abuse of freedom, and its associated behaviour, can be as effective in damaging our relationship with God as trying to follow a set of rules and regulations.

The Churches in Galatia seem to have used their concept of freedom as an excuse to say what they liked about anybody, regardless of whether it was hurtful or not (see verse 15). Continuing to behave in this manner, Paul suggests, will act like a magnet and encourage other forms of destructive behaviour.

Just as Paul writes that trying to live by rules and regulations (the law) makes Christ's death pointless, he also points out that claiming to be followers of Jesus Christ and then behaving in a way that goes against everything that Jesus taught is not the best way to please God either.

By claiming to have faith in Jesus Christ, the Galatian Christians had access to God at all times through the Holy Spirit. This allowed a two-way communication process: the Christians could express their thoughts to God and he could share his thoughts with them. If the Galatians were willing to listen, then they could be guided by the Holy Spirit in all their actions. The result of ignoring this communication process was to allow selfish desires to direct behaviour and make it difficult to obey Christ's command to 'love others as much as you love yourself' (verse 14).

Nothing changes. Paul could have been writing the same letter to Christians today. We know how God would like us to behave but sometimes we act as if we've never read or heard of Jesus' command to love one another. Continually allowing our own desires to cloud our judgement only succeeds in making us feel as if we're a million miles away from God. He loves us and knows that we find it difficult to act as he wants all the time. The best way to avoid causing hassle for ourselves and others is to chat with God about situations. So, let's keep chatting and allow God's Spirit to guide us.

36

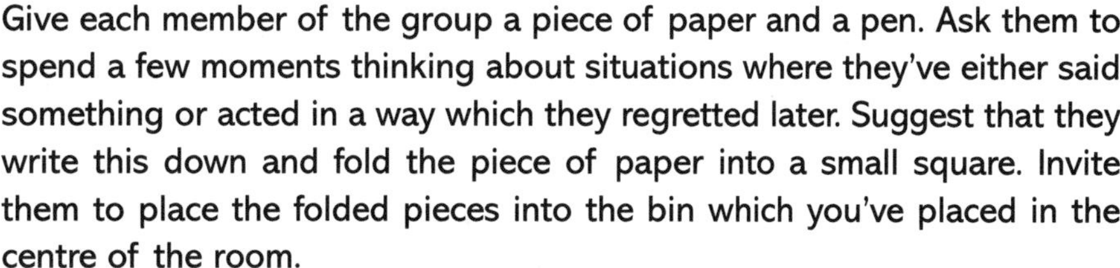

Give each member of the group a piece of paper and a pen. Ask them to spend a few moments thinking about situations where they've either said something or acted in a way which they regretted later. Suggest that they write this down and fold the piece of paper into a small square. Invite them to place the folded pieces into the bin which you've placed in the centre of the room.

Without going into any personal detail, encourage some of the group to talk about other situations which have caused them to feel uncomfortable and made them want to react in a way which they know isn't the way God would have them choose.

(Allow 5 minutes.)

With all the pieces of paper placed in the wastepaper bin, ask the group to be quiet for a few moments while you read the following prayer:

Lord,
  here I am,
  saying sorry, again,
  for behaving like a cranky gorilla
  at a toddlers' tea party.
I didn't mean to make anyone feel
  as if they belonged
  on another planet –
  or even suggest that they should
  see a vet.
You know how it is,
  one thing leads to another
  and before you know it,
  bang! I've shot my mouth off,
  again.
I wouldn't mind so much,
  but I always feel so guilty
  afterwards.
As if I've stolen something.
Maybe I have –
  stolen something –
  like another person's
  happiness,
  or their confidence.
As if I've screwed it up
  and tossed it away like garbage.
I'm sorry, please help me.
Can we start again, like I know we should?

TODAY'S SPECIAL

Holding out my hand

Galatians 6:(1-6) 7-16: Help each other

Equipment:
paper and pens
music and lyrics or drama sketch

Ask the group to stand in a circle (if you have a large group, two circles). Ask each group member to hold their hands out, at waist level, and, with their right hand, grasp the hand of the person on their left and with their left hand, grasp the hand of the person on their right. If they've done this correctly, everyone in the circle should be joined together. The object of the game is to try and uncross everyone's hands without letting go of their partner's hands. At the finish, everyone should still form a circle and remain joined together, but with their hands at their sides.

This can be a difficult game and may not be easy for any group members who have a problem with mobility.

(Allow 10 minutes for this activity.)

Helping each other to solve a problem can be fun but it can also be extremely frustrating. Take a look at 'Through the cross' by Mike Burn (*The source new songs*, 71) or 'O, your hands of kindness' by Martin Smith (*The source new songs*, 54). Alternatively, you might like to use the drama sketch *The Wrinklies go gardening* (see page 149).

(Allow approximately 5 minutes.)

It can be difficult to see what other people are doing when you are desperately trying look where you're going!

Read Galatians 6:(1-6) 7-16.

Paul has spent most of his letter to the Churches in Galatia telling them that they shouldn't listen to those people who insist that God wouldn't be interested in anyone who didn't uphold the Jewish Law. These Judaizers were saying that everyone who considered themselves followers of Jesus Christ should be circumcised as an outward expression of their desire to serve God. Paul was incensed that anyone should listen to the Judaizers. In fact, he goes as far as to say that these troublemakers should not only be circumcised, but have much more cut off as well! (see Galatians 5:12).

Those who were causing problems for the Christians by advocating following strict rules and regulations were certainly not, in Paul's view, of much encouragement to any of the Christians. If anything, the Judaizers were not only causing problems by putting obstacles in the way of believers, but also encouraging them to go the wrong way. No wonder that Paul suggested such drastic surgery for the troublemakers!

Rather than get all confused and wrapped up in problems, Paul was trying to persuade the Galatian Christians to watch out for each other, not to stand idle and watch each other get into all sorts of trouble.

The Galatian Christians had plenty of hassles. Not only were they having their ears bent by those who wanted them to conform to a set of rules, but they had problems with dodgy relationships, scandals, gossip and superstition. The problems are much the same for many people today. It is so easy to get involved with all kinds of things that end up causing us grief. A momentary indiscretion, or a slip of the tongue, can quickly find us stomping around in an emotional sewer.

Paul made it clear that anybody can come up against an obstacle that they find too difficult to deal with by themselves. Nobody should think that they are better than others at dealing with problems. Everybody has a responsibility to help others and not be too busy trying to impress people. God knows how hard some things are to deal with and he doesn't want anyone to pretend that they can deal with things on their own. There are two key points that Paul emphasises. First, if anyone is finding life tough going, then they should be honest and tell someone the problem. Second, people shouldn't be too quick to point the finger and gossip about other people's problems. Rather than indulge in a bit of character assassination, make an effort to help and avoid making somebody's life a misery. Life is tough enough without piling on the agony by pointing out another person's failure. We're all likely to come up against situations which cause us problems, and then we may be glad of a little help.

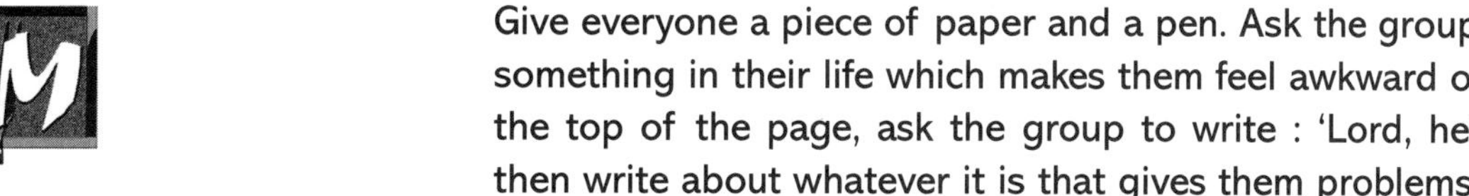

Give everyone a piece of paper and a pen. Ask the group to think about something in their life which makes them feel awkward or depressed. At the top of the page, ask the group to write : 'Lord, help me . . .' and then write about whatever it is that gives them problems.

Ask them to fold the paper and put it away somewhere so that they can refer to it at a later date (preferably somewhere safe so that no one else can read it!). Give each group member another piece of paper and, again, put at the top of the paper: 'Lord, help me . . .' and then write just their name on the paper. Ask anyone who is willing to put their piece of paper onto a notice board which will act as a sort of 'Prayer board', a reminder to pray for those people.

(Allow 5 minutes.)

Ask the group to look at the board and choose someone, not themselves, to pray for. Allow the group a few moments and then suggest that they pray silently for that person. After a short pause, read the following prayer:

Lord,
   you know I've been having a few problems lately.
But there's nothing to worry about,
I'm only up to my ankles
   in the emotional swamp.
I could mention others
   who are not so lucky.
I only hope
   that you've taught them how to swim.
If I'm honest,
   things have been tough for a while.
You know how it is,
   one thing leads to another and . . .
   whoops, it's up to my waist.
There's still nothing to worry about.
I've dealt with this before.
Not too successfully though,
   as you know.
Oh, I seem to have sunk up to my armpits.
Look, this isn't funny.
I'm really trying, you know,
   to keep up appearances
   but it doesn't seem to help.
In fact, it makes matters worse,
   because everyone thinks I'm alright,
   and I'm not.
So, if you've got a moment,
   could you lift me out?
And it would help a lot
   if there was someone else about.

THE WRINKLIES GO GARDENING

Characters Two aged Wrinklies who have had a lifetime of dealing with problems. You'd think with all that experience they'd have everything sorted by now . . . !

Scene The aged grumps are standing at the edge of a vegetable plot. Old 1 has had a hard day digging and planting and isn't too happy about some of the advice being offered by Old 2.

Props knotted handkerchiefs
garden hoe
two glasses of juice

Old 1 *(Wipes forehead and takes drink from glass)* Phew, it's been a hard day's work. *(Leans on hoe)*

Old 2 *(Takes drink from glass)* Tell me about it.

Old 1 What do you mean 'tell me about it', you've only just arrived.

Old 2 I had to walk here.

Old 1 So?

Old 2 It's hot.

Old 1 I'd noticed.

Old 2 There you are then.

Old 1 *(Bangs hoe onto the ground)* You wouldn't know what an honest day's work is.

Old 2 Don't start getting all high and mighty with me. You're only putting these plants in because they've put the price of vegetables up at the local store.

Old 1 Well, no sense in throwing money away.

Old 2 That would be a first for you.

Old 1 My mum always used to say, 'Look after the little coins and the big ones will look after themselves.'

Old 2 I thought it was something to do with little acorns and big oak trees?

Old 1 You'd look daft trying to pay your grocery bill with acorns.

Old 2 You could always suggest they invest them, you know, plant 'em and see what happens.

Old 1 I don't think they're that patient.

Old 2 You'd better be if you expect to get anything to grow where you've planted that lot.

Old 1 What do you mean?

Old 2 Well, for instance, who's ever heard of putting those plants there. *(Points to an area of the vegetable plot)*

Old 1 Nothing wrong with where I've put 'em.

Old 2 Not a lot right either.

Old 1 Hey, if you've come to pick fault you can go somewhere else and offer your useless advice there.

Old 2 No need to get shirty.

Old 1 It's been a tough day. I'm all sweaty, I've got dirty fingernails and I'm embarrassed.

Old 2 I'd be embarrassed if I'd put those plants where you've put them.

Old 1 It's nothing to do with the plants.

Old 2 So why are you embarrassed?

Old 1 I spent 20 minutes trying to pull the wrinkles out of my socks this morning.

Old 2 Nothing to get embarrassed about.

Old 1 I wasn't wearing any.

Old 2 *(Nods head)* That's age for you.

Old 1 Age has nothing to do with it.

Old 2 Of course it does.

Old 1 Age only matters if you're a cheese.

Old 2 *(Prods Old 1 in ribs)* Gravity taking its toll?

Old 1 What are you on about?

Old 2 *(Prods Old 1 in ribs again)* Plenty of pudding there.

Old 1 *(Strokes ribs)* Nothing wrong with a bit of padding, keeps the cold out.

Old 2 There's enough padding there to stuff a sofa.

Old 1 Is this all you've got to do all day, criticise other people?

Old 2 Only pointing out the truth.

Old 1 It's rude to point.

Old 2 *(Mockingly)* Ooooh, can't take a simple comment, eh?

Old 1 *(Annoyed)* Look, age is where a narrow waist and a broad mind swap places, understand?

Old 2 That's a bit philosophical for this time of the day, isn't it?

Old 1 I'm only being honest.

Old 2 So was I.

Old 1 You expressed an opinion, I made an observation.

Old 2 So, what's the difference?

Old 1 You picked fault with me, I made an observation that wasn't aimed at any particular individual.

Old 2 *(Takes another drink of juice and then grunts)* Uh!

Old 1 You don't like it when somebody else is right, do you?

Old 2 It isn't a question of right and wrong, it's all about somebody, and I won't mention names, who gets too picky.

Old 1 You don't like the truth, that's your problem. *(Hoes ground)*

Old 2 *(Points to a spot a short distance away)* You've missed a weed.

Old 1 *(Lifts hoe and looks directly at Old 2)* Oh no, I haven't.

TODAY'S SPECIAL

Chatting to the sky

Colossians 1:1-14: A prayer of thanks

Equipment:
handout and pens
large envelope
music and lyrics

Give each group member a copy of the following handout.

1. I think I'm . . .
   A. too easily influenced by other people
   B. pushy
   C. stubborn
   D. a chocolate addict
   E. a real fruit and nut
2. Sometimes I . . .
   A. say far too much
   B. don't say enough
   C. eat too many peanuts
   D. put my foot in it
   E. daren't say what I'm thinking
3. If I had the chance I'd . . .
   A. tell somebody exactly what I thought of them
   B. say sorry
   C. not do that again
   D. eat more raspberry jam
   E. try and be more positive
4. I . . .
   A. think I'm OK
   B. could do with a paper bag over my head
   C. want to learn to knit woolly socks
   D. shouldn't be so hard on myself
   E. need a bit of ego deflating
5. I think praying is . . .
   A. a waste of time
   B. talking to myself
   C. making me fall asleep
   D. a relationship with God
   E. for emergencies only

Ask the group to tick the response which they feel is most appropriate to them. They may feel like adding their own response. Encourage the group to be as honest as possible.

(Allow 10 minutes for this activity.)

Being honest with ourselves can be both frightening and revealing. Being honest with other people is definitely frightening. Being honest with God is something else!

Take a look at 'Better by far' by Mark Altrogge (*The source new songs*, 6) or 'Create in me a pure heart' by Sue Howson (*The source new songs*, 8).

(Allow approximately 5 minutes.)

Saying what we really think can sometimes be too much for another person to deal with. But saying what we think to God is the type of honesty that he wants.

Read Colossians 1:1-14.

Talking about prayer is one of the best ways to make people think you're either doing OK in your relationship with God or that you are about ready for a trip to the psychiatrist. Prayer usually gets a reaction, one way or the other!

Prayer, or chatting with God, is a great way to say what you think and share your concerns without being judged by others. God genuinely wants to hear what we think and encourages us to express our feelings to him. When we're happy, tell him about it; when we're worried, tell him about it.

It isn't always easy to be honest with your friends and family. Some things that concern us feel a bit too personal or embarrassing to share with people. It's good to develop relationships with people who you know you can trust and whose opinion you respect, although this can take time; even then some things can be difficult to talk about.

Chatting with God is also a good way of thanking him for our friends and family, or expressing our appreciation for something that has happened. The best thing about prayer is that we can be real, say what we think. God would rather hear what bothers us than only get the occasional chat when everything is OK. So, however you feel, God's got an ear for you.

Ask the group to look again at some of their responses to the questions on the handout.

- Are there some areas of their lives that they find difficult to accept?
- Do they find it hard to express their feelings about these issues?
- Do they find it difficult to chat with God?

Ask the group to write down what they think on the back of the handout. **(Allow 5 minutes.)**

Have a large envelope ready. Ask the group to place their handouts in the envelope. Write on the front of the envelope, in large letters: TO GOD. Place the envelope on the floor in front of the group. Suggest to the group that they might like to be quiet for a few moments and chat to God about some of the things they find difficult in their lives. After a short time read the following:

Psalm 5:1-8, 11-12.
Listen Lord, as I pray!
Pay attention when I groan.
You are my King and my God.
Answer my cry for help because I pray to you.
Each morning you listen to my prayer,
  as I bring my requests to you
  and wait for your reply.
You are not the kind of God who is pleased with evil.
Sinners can't stay with you.
No one who boasts can stand in your presence, Lord,
  and you hate evil people.
You destroy every liar,
  and you despise violence and deceit.
Because of your great mercy,
  I come to your house, Lord,
  and I am filled with wonder as I bow down
  to worship at your holy temple.
You do what is right, and I ask you to guide me.
Make your teaching clear because of my enemies . . .
Let all who run to you for protection
  always sing joyful songs.
Provide shelter for those who truly love you
  and let them rejoice.
Our Lord, you bless those who live right,
  and you shield them with your kindness.

TODAY'S SPECIAL

Don't give up!

Colossians 1:15-28: The person and work of Christ

Equipment:
flipchart
paper and pens
music and lyrics

Ask the group to sit in a circle with two chairs back to back in the centre of the circle. Ask for two volunteers: one to be a counsellor, the other to be a telephone caller with a problem. Choose one of the scenarios below and ask the two volunteers to act out their roles. The telephone caller explains their problem and the counsellor offers some advice. The caller can add to or question any of the advice that the counsellor offers.

At an appropriate moment, end the role-play and ask the rest of the group what they thought of the advice.

Scenario 1
It's next door's dog. It barks all day and whines all night. The people next door go out to work and leave the dog on its own. When they arrive home after work, they let the dog out into the garden and it goes mental. It runs around, barking, jumping up at the fence and growls if any of us go into our garden.

Scenario 2
It's exam time again. I've tried my best to revise but it's been really difficult to find enough time to study all the subjects. I've tried talking to some of my friends but they seem too busy to spend any time chatting. I've even taken some of my revision books with me to my part-time job at the local store. The trouble is, it's very busy most of the time and I rarely get the chance to take a break and look at my books.

Scenario 3
It's this boy/girl at school/college. I think they're the best thing I've seen since banana and custard. I'd like to let them know how I feel but I'm too embarrassed. What if they don't feel the same way? Yesterday someone told me that this boy/girl has got a dodgy reputation. They expect you to go all the way on the first date.

The group discussion should try to look at the situation from both sides. What would the group do if they found themselves in a similar situation?

(Allow 10 minutes for this activity.)

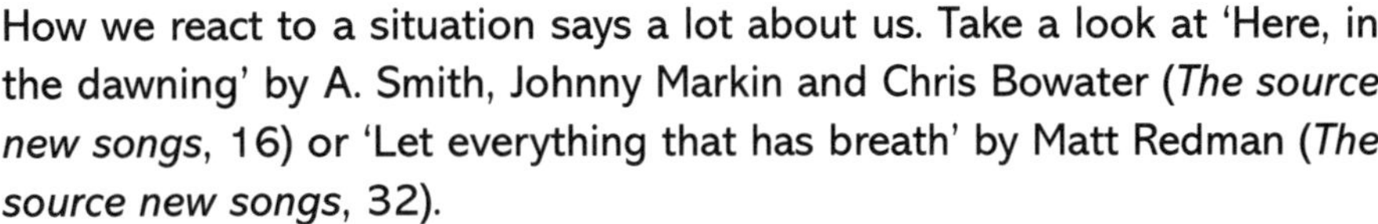

How we react to a situation says a lot about us. Take a look at 'Here, in the dawning' by A. Smith, Johnny Markin and Chris Bowater (*The source new songs*, 16) or 'Let everything that has breath' by Matt Redman (*The source new songs*, 32).

(Allow approximately 5 minutes.)

Did any of the group find the role-play difficult? Was any of the advice relevant? Is it possible to avoid confrontation?

Read Colossians 1:15-28.

The one thing the Church in Colossae didn't lack was advice. Opinions flew from everywhere, giving differing advice and often causing more problems than they solved!

At the time of writing the letter to Colossae, Paul was in prison. He hadn't had the opportunity to visit the Christians at Colossae but had heard about some of the problems they were trying to deal with.

The town of Colossae was quite small but located in a beautiful area that attracted people from other regions and countries. The Church members included local people, Greeks, and Jews. Although everyone in the Church claimed to be followers of Jesus Christ, this didn't stop them referring to customs and practices that were part of everyday life within their original culture. There were those who thought it wrong to enjoy life and so refused to own or do anything that would make their life pleasurable (Ascetics). There were Jews who, although encouraging belief in Jesus Christ, also recommended obeying rituals and practices that let everyone know that you were trying to be religious. There were also people who believed that their life was governed by angelic beings who controlled the destiny of every human.

So, you can imagine all the differing advice and opinions that would form part of any discussion.

This is precisely why Paul started his letter by writing a list of Christ's credentials. It was important to remind the Christians in Colossae of Christ's character and authority. Christ wasn't to be referred to as someone who made people live like slaves to a set of rules and regulations or as a tyrant who could only be satisfied when people deprived themselves of any sort of enjoyment. Most importantly, Paul wanted to make sure that everyone understood that 'everything seen and unseen, including all powers, and all rulers and authorities' (verse 16), only existed because God created everything.

Rather than have a faith that was a mixture of truth, superstition and slavery to lists of rules, Paul encouraged the Christians to live according to everything they had originally heard and believed about Jesus Christ.

Today we have the same problems. We are surrounded by 'advisors' who say our lives are governed either by the stars, aliens, crystals, obedience to strict regulations, animal spirits, stone objects or by ourselves.

The writing of Paul still encourages us to appreciate that some people will believe that their lives are ruled by odd beliefs and practices, but the bottom line is that everything is less than God. He is the creator and the only power that controls the universe and everything beyond. The very same God made the ultimate sacrifice to make sure that we could have a one-to-one relationship with him. Not a relationship based on rules or superstition, but one based upon love.

Ask the group what they think about fortune-telling, star signs and other forms of getting 'advice'.

- Are there any problems with relying on this type of 'guidance'?
- How do using other forms of 'guidance' affect our belief in God?
- What does Paul recommend we should do? (see verse 23).

Using a flipchart, ask the group to recommend ways which will encourage each of us 'not to give up'. For example, chat with God, read the Bible, chat with friends, share any difficulties with people we respect, check out worship, meet with other Christians.

Ask the group to spend a few moments being quiet while you read the following:

Psalm 100.
Shout praises to the Lord, everyone on this earth.
Be joyful and sing as you come in to worship the Lord!
You know the Lord is God!
He created us, and we belong to him;
    we are his people, the sheep in his pasture.
Be thankful and praise the Lord
    as you enter his temple.
The Lord is good!
His love and faithfulness will last for ever.

TODAY'S SPECIAL

Free to walk

Colossians 2:6-15: Christ brings real life

Equipment:
six postcards
candle
music and lyrics

Write one of the descriptions below on each postcard.

1. To increase spending, large retail companies spray all paper money with an invisible substance that reacts with human skin to produce an irritation. The result is that we have an overwhelming desire to get rid of the irritant (money) as quickly as possible.
2. If you stare at the sky long enough you can make it go dark.
3. The Government is thinking of introducing square wheels on all vehicles as an alternative to spending large amounts of money on traffic calming road 'humps'. It is also hoped that the square wheel will reduce the number of deaths caused by speeding vehicles.
4. Staring at a clock will cause it to slow down.
5. A well-known furniture store is to introduce a tubular, floor-mounted filing system. People will be able to store all their documents simply by dropping them into the opening at the top of the tube. All the documents will then be sorted automatically by a small photo-sensitive device which files each document alphabetically.
6. A new computerised oven is about to appear in selected stores. The new ovens will be able to inform you of the number of calories your food contains and suggest an alternative recipe using non-fattening ingredients.

Give the cards to group members who can talk freely without getting tongue-tied. The idea is for one group member at a time to persuade the other group members that the statement written on their card is true.

(Allow 10 minutes for this activity.)

How can we ever sort out the jumble of words which all claim to be the 'truth'?

Take a look at 'Love songs from heaven' by Noel and Tricia Richards (*The source new songs*, 41) or 'O sacred King' by Matt Redman (*The source new songs*, 50).

(Allow approximately 5 minutes.)

We are often presented with half-truths and guesses dressed up as facts. Confusion will almost certainly cause us to stand still and wonder which way is forward.

Read Colossians 2:6-15.

TV chat shows, documentaries, books and newspapers thrive on details which are sensational, radical, stunning and amazing. It doesn't matter whether the details are true or not. In fact, the lack of real facts allows the 'details' to be enhanced by suggestion and imagination.

Many people have said one thing to the media only for the truth to be revealed at a later date. We are given various promises by politicians, sales personnel, philosophers and religious leaders. Everyone claims to be able to deliver their promises or know someone to blame if things don't turn out the way they'd hoped. If someone offers hope in what looks like a hopeless situation, most people would rather be optimistic and cling to the promise of better things. All these things are really like the froth on a cappuccino or the icing on a cake; the appearance leads us to believe in a substance underneath which is not there.

Paul encourages every Christian to let Christ be the foundation of their lives. If we develop our relationship with God and gauge everything we see and hear by what we know to be God's heart for us (best expressed in the Bible), then we will not feel trapped by the deafening roar of those shouting for our attention. The best way to avoid confusion is to let God join us in our everyday lives. That's got to be a whole lot better than running in circles and trying to follow a crowd of different voices shouting for attention.

Ask the group if it's possible to believe everything they read in the newspapers and see on the TV.

- How can we know who's telling the truth and who's trying to fool us?
- Have the group any suggestions or a 'check-list' that might be useful in helping everyone recognise the difference between truth, half-truth and fiction?

(Allow 5 minutes.)

Place a candle in the centre of the room. Ask the group to be quiet for a while. Light the candle and read the following prayer:

Lord,
I often feel as if I'm standing
  in the middle of a football crowd.
The deafening roar
  hurts my ears
  and makes my head ache.
Sometimes it seems as if I'm in a dark tunnel
  without a light.
I can't see where I've been
  or where I should go.
I'm not too sure
  about putting my feet down
  when I can't see
  what I might be stepping in.
And then there are the really bad times
  when the football crowd
  have joined me in the tunnel
  and now I can't hear a thing
  or see anything,
  and no one can hear me shout.
But you, Lord,
  can perform miracles.
You can make yourself heard
  above the deafening noise,
  be seen in the darkest night,
  and can hear me when I whisper.
Be with me,
  teach me,
  listen to me,
  as my heart beats to the rhythm
  of the creator of the universe.

TODAY'S SPECIAL

Wake up!

Colossians 3:1-11: New life with Christ

Equipment:
paper and pens
flipchart
egg-timer
music and lyrics

Give each member of the group a piece of paper and a pen. Write the following categories on the flipchart and ask the group to calculate how many minutes/hours each week they spend on each category.

Watching TV	Listening to music	Eating cereal
Having a shower	Eating chocolate	Picking fluff from between toes
Brushing teeth	Chewing gum	Staring out of window
Putting shoes on	Sleeping	

Compare notes between the group. You might like to calculate the time for each category in a month/year/decade.

(Allow 10 minutes for this activity.)

It can come as a surprise to find out how much time we spend on activities that appear inconsequential.

Have a look at 'Beautiful Lord, wonderful Saviour' by Darlene Zschech (*The source new songs*, 4) or 'Come, now is the time to worship' by Brian Doerksen (*The source new songs*, 7).

(Allow approximately 5 minutes.)

You might define time as the distance between where you are now and where you want to be. How we get there and what we do on the journey is life.

Read Colossians 3:1-11.

If you knew exactly how long you had to live, would it make any difference to the way you live? Would you write a list of things you wanted to do and set about achieving them or would you simply tick the days off on a calendar?

Perhaps it's better that we don't really know what our lifespan is going to be. But it does raise the question of what we do with our time. It can be quite frightening to calculate precisely how much time we spend doing everyday things such as eating, sleeping, watching TV and even cleaning our teeth. Once you've worked out how much time you spend on these activities you may wonder if you've any time left to do anything else!

In his letter to the Church in Colossae, Paul discusses a range of things that people find to occupy their time! He acknowledges that most people are faced with situations which can be extremely difficult to deal with. Sometimes an issue suddenly erupts which causes us to react in such a way that, later, we are annoyed with ourselves over the way we behaved. At other times it is alarming to see how much time and energy we waste getting mixed up in messy situations we should have avoided in the first place.

The problem is what we allow to occupy, or control, our lives. It can be depressing to think about the amount of time we spend behaving in a way that causes tension or anger between ourselves and our friends and family. At times we are not really aware that our behaviour is having a negative affect on people around us. Nobody is perfect, but we do have the ability to consider and think about the way we are behaving.

If we ignore the way we behave and dismiss it as something that just 'happens', then we are also ignoring everything that God has to say about life. Sooner or later our behaviour becomes a 'way of life', a habit that starts to dictate how we spend our time. Paul encourages the Christians in Colossae to 'wake up' – it doesn't have to be this way. In the same way we are encouraged to 'wake up' and make the most of our lives rather than suddenly wonder where the time went.

Using the same piece of paper from the 'Nibbles' section, ask the group to try and work out how much time they have spent in the last week arguing, sulking, moaning or gossiping. Encourage the group to be honest with themselves.

- Are they surprised with the results?
- Were any of these incidents avoidable?
- How can we avoid 'wasting' time occupied in a form of behaviour which is destructive to relationships?

(Allow 5 minutes.)

Place an egg-timer in the centre of the room. Ask the group how they would feel if they had to watch an egg-timer constantly for two days. Would it make them aware of time passing? Would they alter the way they behaved or what they tried to achieve?

Turn the egg-timer so that it starts to empty its contents into the bottom section. Ask the group to be quiet and to think of any issues or situations that they consider to have had a negative affect on their lives and the people around them. Wait until the egg-timer has finished and then read the following:

Psalm 37:39-40.
The Lord protects his people,
    and they can come to him in times of trouble.
The Lord helps them and saves them from the wicked
    because they run to him.'

TODAY'S SPECIAL

Where are we going?

Hebrews 11:1-3, 8-16: God's gallery of faith

Equipment:
postcards
pens
flipchart
bowl and small plastic bag
music and lyrics

Give every member of the group a postcard and a pen. Ask them to write a question beginning with the word *why*. Collect the cards. Hand out a second card and ask everyone to write an answer on the card that begins with *because*. Collect the cards in and shuffle them. Distribute one *why* card and one *because* card to each person and ask them to read out the question followed by the answer – which should produce some odd results!

(Allow 10 minutes for this activity.)

Most of us have many questions that we'd like to have answered. Sometimes the answer can make us wonder whether we asked the right question!

Take a look at 'I trust in you, my faithful Lord' by Darlene Zschech (*The source new songs*, 25) or 'You're the one who flung the stars' by Mark Altrogge (*The source new songs*, 82). Alternatively, you might like to use the drama sketch *The Wrinklies discuss curves* (see page 168).

(Allow approximately 5 minutes.)

There's a sort of security in knowing the answers, but does that mean we should feel insecure if we don't know the answer to a specific question?

Read Hebrews 11:1-3, 8-16.
What happens when we run out of answers? What do we do when we've been going along in a certain direction, quite happily, and then suddenly something halts our progress? Quite often, in those circumstances, we will ask someone who does know the answer or speak to someone who has 'been there' before.

When we were young we often learnt how to do certain things by watching other people and then mimicking their actions. As we grew older we wanted to know more than simply 'how' to do things, we wanted to know 'why?' 'Why does this happen when I do that?' or 'Why doesn't this work?' Again, we would be shown how or how not to do certain things but this time with an additional explanation. Slowly we developed an understanding and an appreciation of why things happen the way they do and how we can respond to the situation. Eventually, it may be our turn to do the explaining and answering the 'whys'.

The writer to the Hebrews starts to explain what's required in situations where we feel insecure. The writer says what we need is to feel secure in our insecurity! What we need is *faith*. Straightaway we are at a disadvantage: what on earth is *faith*?

The answer lies in being able to appreciate how other people have responded to situations by their faith in God; then we can say, 'OK, God, that's how it was for them, now it's my turn'.

The Bible contains many examples of how different people from different backgrounds and cultures have acted 'in faith'. Faith isn't a substance that can be moulded into something that we can see. It has no form or shape that allows us to take a handful off the shelf and throw it at a situation. We can often see the results of faith but not always instantaneously. Sometimes it takes a while for things to happen and we get annoyed and wonder what God is messing about at. The trouble is, we can't see the whole picture. We don't exist in isolation and God is often sorting things out for us and for other people because our actions affect other people as much as their actions affect us.

As we begin to see the results of placing our faith in God, we are surprised that what we expected to be a simple answer turns out to be far more wonderful than we ever imagined.

Faith is putting our trust in God. Sometimes God responds by providing us with a quick 'snack', something that encourages us and deals with our immediate needs. At other times God responds by providing an enormous meal which keeps us going for a long time. These bigger 'meals' take a bit longer to prepare but the wait is worth it.

We can be encouraged by other people's faith and we can encourage people by our faith. There is not a process or formula by which we can apply a dab of faith to a problem. Faith is trusting God and knowing that he has everything under control.

Write the word 'Faith' onto the flipchart. Ask the group whether they think faith is simply wishful thinking: if we wait long enough something will happen. If we can't see or feel faith as a tangible object, how can we know it has any effect?

Write down some of their comments on the flipchart.

(Allow 5 minutes.)

Place a bowl in the centre of the room. Take a small plastic bag out of your pocket and pretend to pour the contents into the bowl. Explain to the group that you have just put some top grade air into the bowl. Don't try to convince the group of your sanity, it would take far too long!

Faith is like air. We know it exists because without it the effects are extremely visible! Air helps us to function in the way we were created to function. Faith is pretty much the same.

Ask the group to be quiet while you read the following:

From Psalm 139.
You have looked into my heart, Lord,
  and you know all about me.
You know when I am resting or when I am working,
  and from heaven you discover my thoughts.
You notice everything I do and everywhere I go.
Before I even speak a word
  you know what I will say,
  and with your powerful arm
  you protect me from every side.
I can't understand all this!
Such wonderful knowledge is far above me . . .
Your thoughts are far beyond my understanding,
  much more that I could ever imagine.
I try to count your thoughts,
  but they outnumber the grains on the beach.
And when I awake, I will find you nearby . . .
Look deep into my heart, God,
  and find out everything I am thinking.
Don't let me follow evil ways,
  but lead me in the way that time has proved true.

THE WRINKLIES DISCUSS CURVES

Characters	Two aged grumps who lift their thoughts to higher things, even though they had to start at the bottom and argue their way to the top.
Scene	The two Wrinklies are sitting on a bench. Old 1 has a smug grin on his face, while Old 2 is frustrated at not being able to find out what's going on.
Props	bench two walking sticks

Old 2 What are you looking so smug about?

Old 1 *(Smirks and looks into the distance)* Nothing.

Old 2 Don't tell me that. You look like the cat that's had the cream, the fish paste and the trifle.

Old 1 *(Leans head to one side and smiles)* It's a nice day.

Old 2 That's beside the point. Normally you only comment about the weather when your knees are playing up.

Old 1 Accurate to a twitch are my knees. I can tell you when rain's due better than any weather forecaster.

Old 2 Is it only rain you can forecast?

Old 1 Oh no, if there's a heatwave on the way my feet throb something awful. If it's going to be stormy my stomach feels as if there's a storm in there. If there's going to be thunder, my head feels as if there's thunder inside it . . .

Old 2 *(Interrupts)* I don't want to know what happens if it's going to be windy.

Old 1 Only explaining, that's all.

Old 2 Well, explain what you're so smug about.

Old 1 *(Places both hands on walking stick and leans forward)* Wouldn't you like to know!

Old 2 I wouldn't be asking if I wasn't interested.

Old 1 Sure you want to know?

Old 2 Are you sure you want to keep breathing?

Old 1 I only struggle for breath if I eat onions. Block me pipes up, they do.

Old 2 Onions are not the only things that make you gasp for breath.

Old 1 What do you mean?

Old 2 Remember when you had to open your purse to pay for that new pair of sandals? That made you gasp for breath.

Old 1 Well, the cost, it was an extortionate price for a simple pair of sandals.

Old 2 It happens every time. Open your purse and your mouth opens, gasping for breath.

Old 1 An involuntary reaction, nothing more.

Old 2 Talking about an involuntary reaction – am I going to have to force the information out of you?

Old 1 Calm down, calm down. Nothing to get your wrinkles agitated about.

Old 2 Tell me what you're so smug about then.

Old 1 *(Takes deep breath and looks proud)* I've made a boat.

Old 2	*(Opens and closes mouth like a fish)* . . . What?
Old 1	Thought you'd be impressed.
Old 2	Impressed? I'm impressed you've got the nerve to try and build anything. Ask you to put a shelf up and the wall looks like it's been attacked by a herd of rhinos.
Old 1	Cheek! You're just jealous, that's what you are.
Old 2	Jealous? How could anybody be jealous of something you've built?
Old 1	The *Happy Wave* is a piece of craftsmanship.
Old 2	Excuse me, did you say the *Happy Wave*?
Old 1	Sure did. That's the name I'm going to give the boat.
Old 2	Is that the *Happy Wave* that washes over your feet after the boat has sunk?
Old 1	Mock all you like. That boat is state of the art.
Old 2	I agree, it would have been a thousand years ago.
Old 1	You'll eat your words when you see the sweet lines and pleasing curves of the boat.
Old 2	I'd prefer to look at the pleasing curves of . . .
Old 1	*(Interrupts)* And there's no need for that kind of talk. You're all talk and no action.
Old 2	*(Leans on walking stick and wobbles the stick)* Give me half a chance . . .
Old 1	*(Interrupts again)* You don't move fast enough to catch a cold. You wait until you see the boat as it bobs gracefully on the waves, the sun illuminating the ample curves of the hull, the shapeliness of the bow . . .

Old 2 *(Wobbles walking stick)* Stop talking like that, it gets me all bothered. *(Takes deep breath)* Anyway, I wouldn't trust that boat of yours to keep my feet dry. I bet it's already half full of water.

Old 1 Typical. You wouldn't climb a mountain because you wouldn't trust it to keep still.

Old 2 A wise precaution. Who'd want to be stuck half-way up a mountain when it decides to throw a wobbly and erupt in your face?

Old 1 So what do you do for fun, watch trees grow?

Old 2 There's worse things in life. It's quite relaxing resting under a tree and being fascinated by the beauty of nature. Mind you, you have to be careful where you sit. People let their dogs make an awful mess on the ground. Can't trust them to do anything properly.

Old 1 The dogs or their owners?

Old 2 Both. People who let their dogs mess everywhere shouldn't be trusted to own a bath sponge.

Old 1 *(Impatiently)* Do you want to see my boat or what?

Old 2 I suppose I'd better. Shall I bring my bath sponge to soak up the water?

TODAY'S SPECIAL

The smile and the frown

Psalm 80:1-2, 8-19: Help our nation

Equipment:
sheets of paper and pens
music and lyrics

Ask the group to write their responses to the following situations. Encourage them to be as honest as they can; no one will be reading their completed sheets. Read out each of the situations below, allowing approximately one minute for the group members to write their response.

1. Recently you told one of your best mates whom you fancied. A couple of days later, not only did half the town know your secret but, worst of all, the object of your desire had also been told.
2. Congratulations, it's your birthday! Aged Aunt Dotty has just given you a present. Your dad whispers that Aunt Dotty hasn't got much money and she had to save up for several weeks to be able to buy your present. When you open it, you discover a pair of furry slippers in a disgusting shade of pink.
3. A letter arrived in this morning's post telling you that you had an interview for a job.
4. Someone told you that today was bad-taste-clothes day and that all the group members would turn up wearing jumble-sale rejects. When you arrive, dressed in your wardrobe's worst, you realise that you've been the butt of a practical joke.
5. You are just looking through one of those top-shelf magazines, purely out of curiosity (!), when someone taps your shoulder. When you turn around your eyes meet those of the vicar.
6. Your family tell you not to worry too much about getting high grades in your exams. When the results come through you have achieved far better grades than anyone thought.

When the group have finished writing their responses, ask each member to fold their piece of paper and put it in their pocket.

(Allow 10 minutes for this activity.)

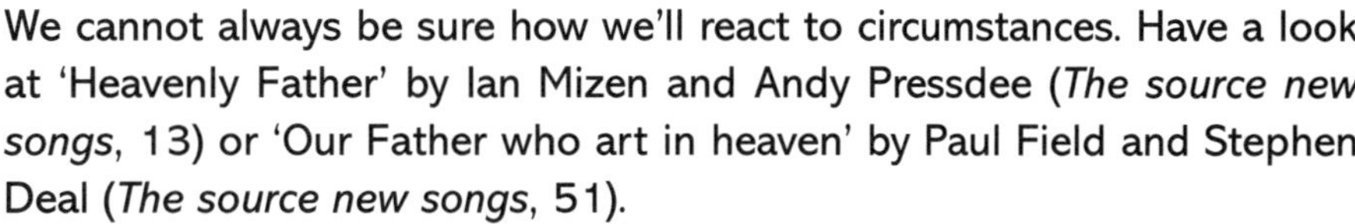

We cannot always be sure how we'll react to circumstances. Have a look at 'Heavenly Father' by Ian Mizen and Andy Pressdee (*The source new songs*, 13) or 'Our Father who art in heaven' by Paul Field and Stephen Deal (*The source new songs*, 51).

(Allow approximately 5 minutes.)

We can rehearse how we'll react to most situations but when it comes to the real thing we may forget everything we have rehearsed.

Read Psalm 80:1-2, 8-19.

The Psalmist begins by reminding himself who God is and what he has done. The main part of the Psalm goes on to list a catalogue of problems and hassles which make the Psalmist feel as if God has taken a holiday.

At least the Psalmist could remember what God had done in the past! Quite often, when we pray, we launch straight in to a list of why this or that shouldn't be happening to us and anyway, why us when so-and-so doesn't even go to church and they never have this problem. Besides, isn't it about time that things improved rather than stayed in a state of sogginess for another millennium?

It's difficult to avoid the barbs of parental persecution or friends' fury. Any possible feeling of guilt is soon snuggling safely under a blanket of self-assured honesty! Even when we feel that the problem wasn't our fault and would never have happened if a 'certain person' had kept their mouth shut, we launch straight in demanding what we want to see happen, rather than reminding ourselves of what God has done in the past.

There is no need to use a bucket load of 'thee', 'thou' and 'therefore'. We can chat with God as we would with our best friend. Would we begin by saying, 'Well, I'm not sure whether you're up to this but . . .'? It's good to remind ourselves about God's character and then chat through the hassle with him. God is the God of the impossible and he just possibly might shock you by doing something about your situation!

Let God put a smile on your face and your frown will turn from one of annoyance to one of amazement at God's love for you.

Ask the group to look again at their 'response' papers. Suggest that they think about some issues they've faced recently or are currently trying to deal with.

- How did they respond?
- Did chatting the situation through with God, either to say thank you or ask what was going on, ever occur to them?

(Allow 5 minutes.)

Ask the group to remain quiet and continue to think about how they respond to issues and situations. While they are quiet, read the following prayer.

Lord,
   was that really necessary?
What on earth were you doing
   while I was trying to deal
   with a truck-load of garbage?
How could this have happened to me?
Why me? Isn't there someone else
   more deserving and better able
   to deal with this emotional sewer material?
I can't believe you let this happen.
One moment I was quietly minding my own business –
   well, that and the occasional verbal assessment
   of someone else's predicament –
   when, all of a sudden,
   I'm up to my neck,
   drowning, slipping, going under,
   sliding and generally
   having the sort of day
   that I'm sure someone else
   would appreciate more than me!
Hey! Don't interrupt.
I only paused for a breath.
Excuse me?
But, but . . .
   oh, yeah, I do remember
   how you helped me
   the last time
   to defy gravity, walk on water
   and turn pigswill into a picnic.
Any chance of a repeat performance?
Sincerely yours . . .

TODAY'S SPECIAL

What's this then?
Psalm 149: A new song of praise

Equipment:
large box
balloon
pin
bag of marshmallows
flipchart
music and lyrics

Before the group arrive, blow up the balloon and place it inside the large box. Close the lid of the box and put the box to one side of the room. Every so often during your explanation of the game and throughout the game, pause, walk over to the box, place your ear to the box and listen. After a few seconds shake your head, tut, and carry on with the game. You must not offer any explanation for either your actions or the box.

On the flipchart draw eleven dashes, one for each letter of the word SCRUMDINGLE. Invite the group, one at a time, to try and guess the letters of the word. If a member suggests a letter that isn't part of the word or one that has already been used, they are given a marshmallow to put in their mouth but *not* to eat. If they get another letter wrong they have a second marshmallow placed in their mouth but they still *cannot* eat the marshmallows.

The more marshmallows in people's mouths, the funnier it is to try and understand what they are saying!

The group can only eat the marshmallows when the word has been completed. Nobody can opt out of the game; everyone, in turn, must try and contribute a letter. When the complete word is revealed the group may argue that such a word doesn't exist – it doesn't, but it sounds like it should and anyway, it's your flipchart . . . so there!

(Allow 10 minutes for this activity.)

We find certain things puzzling and, at times, can't see the point of it. Take a look at 'All around the world' by Paul Oakley (*The source new songs*, 1) or 'Many are the words we speak' by Matt Redman (*The source new songs*, 42).

(Allow approximately 5 minutes.)

Read Psalm 149.

The Psalmist doesn't begin with a simple 'Hello and welcome. Here are the notices . . .' Straightaway everyone is encouraged to 'shout praises to the Lord!' Why?

First, the Psalm suggests that we should feel secure in the knowledge that we have God's love. We are acknowledged as being 'his people' (verses 1-2). Second, there is delight in knowing that we are accepted by the Creator. God has gone out of his way to get to know us. He hasn't laid down a library-load of rules and regulations that we need to follow to gain his acceptance, it's already ours (verse 3). Third, if we include God in our life then he is the one who wants to deal with our hassles and problems. We are not expected to sort things out in isolation. We have God with us and the support and encouragement of other Christians (verses 4-5).

There is nothing that God can't handle. Our relationship with him isn't a bunch of 'maybes' and 'sometimes'. He has promised to do the right thing and be with us even though we may be slithering around in a swamp of hopelessness. God has given his word that he'll walk with us every step of the way. There isn't a place or situation where we'll be alone.

It's also good to remind ourselves of what God has done in the past, whether with us or through the example of people in the Bible (verses 6-7).

Finally, no one gets the better of God. Although we may never understand completely how he operates, we should feel confident that he is in control and will deal with things in his own way (verses 8-9).

With the knowledge that God loves us, will be with us always and will not allow situations to ruin our relationship with him, we have a pretty good reason to start and finish each day with a few words of thanks.

Walk over to the box, place your ear against the lid and listen intently. Stand up, tut and ask the group if they've heard any noises come from the box. Carefully open the lid but don't allow any of the group to look into the box. Put your hands into the box and place them around the balloon. Ask the group to be quiet and listen. When everyone is quiet, take the pin (which you should have hidden either in the box or between your fingers) and burst the balloon.

Ask the group what they thought was in the box before you burst the balloon. Was anyone surprised by the exploding balloon? Explain that although we may not understand some things or may even be puzzled by their existence, it doesn't mean we should ignore them. God is really pleased when we bother to chat with him and it's important to remind ourselves of what God has done and just what he is capable of!

(Allow 5 minutes.)

ALL SAINTS' DAY 44

Ask the group to spend a few moments being quiet. Suggest that they might like to think of some circumstance where they have experienced God getting involved in their life. Read the following:

Psalm 134.
Everyone who serves the Lord, come and offer praises.
Everyone who has gathered in his temple tonight,
lift your hands in prayer towards his holy place
and praise the Lord.
The Lord is the Creator of heaven and earth,
and I pray that the Lord will bless you from Zion.

TODAY'S SPECIAL

Whoops, sorry!

Psalm 32:1-7: The joy of forgiveness

Equipment:
postcards
paper and pens
small cross
music and lyrics or drama sketch

Prepare three postcards for each member of the group. One postcard will have 'Forgive' written on it, the second will have 'Sometime, maybe' written on it and the final card will have 'Never' written on it.

Read the following scenarios to the group and, after each one, ask the group whether they would forgive. Each member of the group will then 'vote' to show how they would respond.

1. Jenny has just telephoned her boyfriend to tell him she's pregnant. He's furious and blames Jenny for not being 'careful'. She apologises but tells him she's sometimes so tired at nights that two or three days can go by without her taking the pill. Her boyfriend slams the phone down. Jenny doesn't hear from him for six weeks. Suddenly, late one night, he telephones and says he's sorry and can she forgive him for reacting the way he did?
2. Tony has been saving for a two-month walking holiday in Scandinavia. He only needs to work at his part-time job for five more weeks and he'll have enough money saved. Just as he's about to leave work one Thursday evening Tony's boss calls him to one side and informs him that because work is slow at the moment he can't afford to employ Tony any longer. Tony's furious and demands that he be allowed to work for the next five weeks as he was promised. The boss refuses. Tony walks home wondering whether he should forgive his boss and go and apologise.
3. Ben is a soccer fanatic. He's just been invited, with his best friend Dan, to go for a trial with a local team. When they arrive at the training ground Ben realises that he's forgotten his soccer boots. He remembers that his friend's boots are the same style and size as his own. While his best friend chats to the coach, Ben opens his friend's bag and takes the soccer boots. Ben plays in the training match while his friend watches from the bench. Ben gets selected to play for the team. His best friend receives a polite 'thanks, but no thanks'. Ben is really happy to get chosen for the team but his friend, although not upset at not getting selected, thinks Ben's behaviour was out of order. He isn't sure how to respond to Ben.

After the group have 'voted' in each scenario, ask them why they chose to vote the way they did.

(Allow 10 minutes for this activity.)

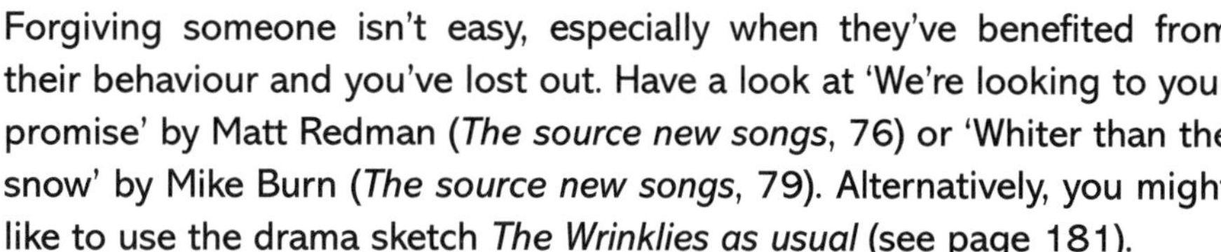

Forgiving someone isn't easy, especially when they've benefited from their behaviour and you've lost out. Have a look at 'We're looking to your promise' by Matt Redman (*The source new songs*, 76) or 'Whiter than the snow' by Mike Burn (*The source new songs*, 79). Alternatively, you might like to use the drama sketch *The Wrinklies as usual* (see page 181).

(Allow approximately 5 minutes.)

How we respond to people who have behaved badly towards us says a lot about us as individuals.

Read Psalm 32:1-7.
God sets the ball rolling by choosing to forgive us for the way we've behaved not only towards him but also towards each other. If God can choose to forgive, surely it's easy for us? Don't you believe it.

The psalmist goes into some detail about how he feels when he's chosen not to forgive someone or he's behaved in a way that is far removed from how God wants him to behave. His behaviour makes him feel totally drained; he can hardly put one foot in front of the other.

Each of us knows how it feels to have things weighing on our mind. The thoughts rattle around our heads until we can't see or think straight. Sleep escapes us and we spend the night going over the events and re-enacting the whole scene until it merges into dreams which continue to torment us. Eventually we wake up feeling as if we never went to bed in the first place. God is only too pleased when, bleary eyed and on our knees through tiredness, we hand over the whole problem and ask him to forgive us. The relief hits us like a bucket of cold water.

None of us is so near perfect that getting things wrong never enters our head. It's easy to get messed up with things that are unhealthy for our hearts and minds, but it's just as easy to prevent all the hassle that accompanies the mess and chat the whole thing through with God.

We all know how we feel when we've got involved in situations that mess our heads up and cause us to feel like the inside of a garbage truck. And, just because we know that feeling, it's important that we don't make other people go through the same trauma. Forgiving somebody doesn't make their actions right but it goes a long way to restoring the relationship and then trying to sort out the difficulty. Don't forget, when you're trying to deal with the hassle, get God involved. You know it makes sense!

Ask the group to think for a while about situations where perhaps they've left things unsaid that should have been said. Are there people whom members of the group need to forgive? Give each group member a piece of paper and a pen. Place the cross in the centre of the room. Ask them to write the initials of that person(s) on a sheet of paper and place it next to the cross.

(Allow 5 minutes.)

Once everyone who wants to has placed their paper next to the cross, ask the group to be quiet while you read the following prayer:

Lord,
  you know I used to be so sure
  that it wasn't ever my fault,
  but now I'm not so sure.
Things seem so complicated,
  so confusing
  that I feel as if I'm on a roundabout,
  can't remember where it started
  and don't know if it's ever going to end.
I know this can't continue,
  life is being wasted
  going around in circles
  getting dizzy.
Help me, Lord,
  to forgive
  and be forgiven.
Help me,
  be with me
  especially when I screw up with such finesse.

THE WRINKLIES AS USUAL

Characters	Two aged grumps who are returning home after a shopping trip. Both are feeling physically and financially exhausted.
Scene	A park bench provides a welcome break in the Wrinklies' journey home. The bags of shopping have been parked at their feet.
Props	park bench three or four bags of 'shopping'

Old 1 *(Kicks bags of shopping)* I hate *(kicks bags again)* I hate shopping.

Old 2 Leaves a bad taste in your mouth.

Old 1 Yeah, like rinsing your dentures in dirty washing-up water.

Old 2 Well, at least we got out of the supermarket safely.

Old 1 Yeah, sometimes you barely escape with your purse intact.

Old 2 *(Winces)* The price of some of those things. Makes your knees go all funny.

Old 1 Turns my stomach. It's not right having to part with hard-earned money. Should be a law against it.

Old 2 I suppose they have to make a living somehow.

Old 1 Thieves normally get put behind bars but that lot at the supermarket get away with robbery every week.

Old 2 *(Nods head in agreement)* Somebody ought to shop them! *(Laughs)*

Old 1 Your jokes get worse each time, just like the prices.

Old 2 Steady, my jokes are always bargain basement.

Old 1 That's where you ought to keep them.

Old 2 What, and deprive you of a chance to moan?

Old 1 What do you mean 'moan'? I've never heard such rubbish.

Old 2 *Rubbish?* If they had an event at the Olympics for moaning you'd be in with the chance of a medal.

Old 1 I only say what's necessary. Anyway, I wouldn't compete in the Olympics.

Old 2 Why's that?

Old 1 Wouldn't be fair.

Old 2 That's true.

Old 1 Couldn't stand in the way of emerging talent.

Old 2 You're all heart, which is more than I can say about the management at the supermarket.

Old 1 *(Sucks in breath)* Oooh, did you see the price of those carrots? Enough to give a donkey indigestion.

Old 2 And the price of cakes nowadays. Scandalous. When I were knee-high to a turnip, you could get ten times as many cakes for that price.

Old 1 Ah, those days have well and truly gone.

Old 2 That's true. At least one thing remains the same.

Old 1 What's that?

Old 2 Can't stand the sight of turnips.

Old 1 Neither can I at those prices.

Old 2 Hey, forget about the prices. Have you forgotten what today is?

Old 1 Course I haven't. How could I forget?

Old 2 Well, did you?

Old 1 *(Looking confused)* Did what?

Old 2 You know.

Old 1 Oh, that. *(Still looks confused)* Course I did.

Old 2 Good. Wouldn't like to forget that.

Old 1 Nor me.

Old 2 Same as last time then?

Old 1 Er?

Old 2 You know, the same as we always use.

Old 1 Erm.

Old 2 You didn't change them, did you?

Old 1 *(Looks at socks)* No.

Old 2 So, what's the problem?

Old 1 *(Raises eyebrows)* I wish I knew.

Old 2 You remembered, didn't you? Tell me you remembered.

Old 1 Told you. Course I did. *(Pauses)* Remembered what?

Old 2 *(Sits upright and frowns)* Today is today, right?

Old 1 *(Speaks slowly)* Yeeees.

Old 2 And today is the day we always get them?

Old 1 *(Slowly)* Hmmm.

Old 2 And we never change them, do we?

Old 1 *(Slowly)* Errrr?

Old 2 The numbers?

Old 1 Numbers?

Old 2 Lottery, remember?

Old 1 Oh, that.

Old 2 Good. Because if you'd forgotten, someone very close to me would die a horrible death.

Old 1 Really? I didn't know your donkey was that poorly. *(Waves lottery ticket)*

Old 2 *(Grabs ticket)* Some things are really unforgivable, you know.

TODAY'S SPECIAL

It wasn't me, honest

Psalm 17:1-9: The prayer of an innocent person

Equipment:
paper and pens
music and lyrics

Give each member of the group a piece of paper and a pen. Ask them to write down what they think the speaker really means in each instance. For example, 'I didn't see you there, honest' might mean 'I was hoping you wouldn't see me' or 'Wasn't it obvious I was trying to avoid you?'. It really doesn't hurt' might mean 'I've got thirty seconds to live' or 'It's less painful having teeth pulled out'.

Sentences:

1. It was a bargain.
2. You look wonderful.
3. This tastes gorgeous.
4. You wouldn't understand.
5. That's a great idea.
6. He/she wasn't my type.

When everyone has finished writing their definitions, read the first sentence and ask each member of the group to read out their definition. Repeat for each of the sentences.

(Allow 10 minutes for this activity.)

Saying one thing and meaning another is one thing, but telling the truth and still no one believes you is really annoying. Take a look at 'We bow down' by Viola Grafstrom (*The source new songs*, 73) or 'O God, you are my God' by Beaker (*The source new songs*, 45).

(Allow approximately 5 minutes.)

46

Honesty is something that most people would say is an important characteristic, that is until someone tells us the truth which we would prefer not to hear.

Read Psalm 17:1-9.

Would we believe the truth if we heard it? It's extremely difficult at times to distinguish between a lie, a half-truth and the truth. It has become almost acceptable to avoid the truth by using all sorts of deception and by being 'economical with the facts'.

We have become so used to being deceived by elaborate adverts or sales techniques that we take for granted that what we see or hear is only partially correct. When politicians speak it is either to try and discredit their political opponents or to cover up the truth by using statistics and deceit. Being stingy with the truth has become a way of life.

So, when we do speak the truth it is easily misunderstood as an attempt to disguise the facts.

The Psalmist had the same problem. Nobody seemed to believe him when he told the truth. He cried out to God, saying that no one would believe him and that only God knew his heart.

This may be a situation some of us are familiar with. We've tried telling the truth but no one believes us! What are the reasons for this? It could be that we have been known, in the past, to confuse truth with fiction, or perhaps we usually only speak to accuse someone else of being a fraud. It could also be that we really dislike someone or a situation so much that we will go to almost any lengths to make the people involved appear corrupt.

The Psalmist had no problem with being up front with God and inviting God to know his heart. We may be able to fool people some of the time but we cannot fool God. Why try? We don't need to use all sorts of tactics to avoid looking dodgy to other people. Even when we are falsely accused of something, we can go to God and say, 'You know my heart. Protect me and please don't let people accuse me when I'm innocent.'

God is always with us in every situation. He's not some overbearing boss who's looking to see you trip over your tongue. God wants you to do the right thing even when everybody tells you you're stupid to act like that. It may seem daft to other people but it's really neat with God.

Ask the group if they've ever found themselves in situations where the truth would cause problems for themselves or other people.

- How should we behave in those situations?
- Should we stay silent?
- Is the truth always the best policy?

Discuss the situations and see what alternatives the group can suggest.

(Allow 5 minutes.)

Ask the group to be quiet for a few moments as you read the following:

Proverbs 10:8-12.
If you have good sense, you will listen and obey;
   if all you do is talk, you will destroy yourself.
You will be safe, if you always do right,
   but you will get caught, if you are dishonest.
Deceit causes trouble,
   and foolish talk will bring you to ruin.
The words of good people are a source of life,
   but evil hides behind the words of the wicked.
Hatred stirs up trouble;
   love overlooks the wrong that others do.

TODAY'S SPECIAL

Justice for all

Psalm 98: The Lord works miracles

Equipment:
postcards
flipchart
candle
music and lyrics

Distribute three postcards to each member of the group. You will have prepared the postcards before the session so that one card reads 'Agree', the second reads 'Disagree' and the third 'Don't know'.

Read each of the following statements and ask the group to respond by using one of the cards provided.

Statements:

1. It's OK to watch soft porn on TV; after all, didn't God create some very attractive bodies?
2. If someone is going to be offensive to other people then there's nothing wrong in being offensive to them.
3. Taking a day or more off work/school is just the same as stealing money from someone.
4. Cheating is OK if nobody finds out.
5. There's nothing wrong with driving at 50 miles an hour in a 30-mile speed limit.
6. It doesn't matter if you keep doing things that you know are dishonest or wrong because God will keep forgiving you.

After the group have voted for each statement, discuss each question and ask individual group members to defend their response.

Try to allow the group to reach a consensus of opinion. Offer your own perspective but don't let it dominate the thinking of the group as a whole.

(Allow 10 minutes for this activity.)

People may disagree on many subjects but having faith in God at least allows us all to look in the same direction.

Take a look at 'Standing in your presence' by Darlene Zschech (*The source new songs*, 59) or 'Lord, let your glory fall' by Matt Redman (*The source new songs*, 39).

(Allow approximately 5 minutes.)

Now and then situations occur which cause confusion or make us feel insecure.

Read Psalm 98.
Sometimes it would be easier if everybody just left us alone and people kept their opinions to themselves. Life would be simpler and far less confusing. The only problem with being left to get on with things is that there's no guarantee that we'll be able to work out the best way to do things.

Unfortunately, life's not straightforward and other people will insist on doing things their own way.

Often we are faced with a situation that leaves us confused. What's the best way to go? How are we expected to react? Why isn't life made simple? Giving us a choice as to how we respond is God's way of giving us a unique gift: freewill.

We know before we put one foot in front of the other that sometimes we are bound to make a wrong choice or act in a way that really gets up someone's nose. But at least we had the freedom to make that choice. The important thing is to try and see our actions from God's point of view. And, if we want to follow God's way, to try to change our behaviour and way of thinking.

The Psalmist states that God has the power to bring justice (see verse 2). Another way of describing 'justice' is 'right actions'. God is able to show us, and support us, so that we can do the right thing. You may argue that it's not much use if one person acts right when they are surrounded by loads of other people acting in a way that's far from 'right'. Your actions may appear to be like a grain of sand on the beach but the beach is made up of grains of sand. Encouraging each other to act in the way God would approve of will in turn encourage others to act in a caring and supportive way.

We are not left alone to try and sort things out. God, the Creator of everything, is with us every step of the way. You may feel as if you stand out because you try and do the right thing, but at least you're in good company.

Ask the group to try and define 'justice' or 'right actions'. Write some of the group's ideas onto the flipchart. Is it possible to identify a type of behaviour or some ideas that will encourage us to try and do the right thing?

(Allow 5 minutes.)

Place the candle in the centre of the room. Light the candle and then ask the group to spend a few moments being quiet. Read the following prayer:

Lord,
  now, I'm really lost here,
  I've no idea which way to go,
  what to do
  or whether to do anything at all.
If I turn left
  I'll upset those on the right,
  and if I turn right
  I'll upset those on the left.
If I move forward
  people will think
  I'm trying to leave them behind
  and if I move back
  people will think
  I'm being evasive.
I try to do the right thing, honest,
  but trying to please
  so many people
  with so many points of view,
  opinions,
  ideas
  (and the occasional plague of stubborn behaviour),
  I'll end up doing the wrong thing
  at the wrong time
  for the wrong people.
I think it's about time
  to get a bit of advice.
The confusion is killing me
  (or I'll be killing someone if this goes on much longer).
So, as the Creator and all that,
  I reckon you might have a few good ideas.
Do you mind sharing some?

TODAY'S SPECIAL

Somewhere to run to

Psalm 46: God is our mighty fortress

Equipment:
small sheets of paper and pens
large sheet of paper shaped like an arrow
dictionary
tacks or sticky tape
music and lyrics

Give each group member a piece of paper and a pen. Ask the group to agree on a definition for 'worry'.

- Is it being soft?
- Is it being scared?
- Is it letting fear get the better of you?
- Is it being realistic about your situation?
- Is it being negative?

It might be worth finding a dictionary definition to share with the group after they have agreed on their definition.

Ask the group to write the agreed definition for 'worry' at the top of their piece of paper. Now ask them to write about an issue or concern that is 'worrying' them at the moment. When they have done this, ask them to fold the piece of paper and tape it to the arrow-shaped piece of paper.

(Allow 10 minutes for this activity.)

What may worry you might not concern someone else. Different things may worry different people but that doesn't make your 'worry' any less significant.

Have a look at 'Holy Spirit, rain down' by Russell Fragar (*The source new songs,* 18) or 'I am yours' by David Gate (*The source new songs*, 21).

(Allow approximately 5 minutes.)

You know how it feels, when you want to crawl and hide away from prying eyes because everything seems to be going wrong and everybody wants to have a go at you. Someone else had experienced the same feelings but had discovered somewhere rather special to crawl away to.

Read Psalm 46.
The Psalmist has written a special song to shout (or rather sing with a bit of a melody) about the fact that God is a mighty fortress where anyone can find shelter.

The Psalms were written at a time when Israel was under constant threat of attack from hostile countries, corrupt politicians displayed their hypocrisy with contempt for the average person and even the king wasn't above having someone killed so that he could take what wasn't rightfully his (see 2 Samuel 11).

Families argued and fought amongst themselves (including the royal family) and wealthy people had to be constantly reminded about their role in looking after the poor. All sound a bit familiar?

The Psalms display the full range of human emotions. One moment everything appears to be great and the next moment it's the pits. One moment the Psalmist writes, 'I will celebrate and be joyful because you, Lord, have saved me' (Psalm 35:9) and the next it's, 'Wake up! Do something, Lord! Why are you sleeping? Don't desert us forever' (Psalm 44:23).

The Psalmist had no problem about being honest with God. There was no confidence in any of the systems – social, religious or political – which were controlled by human hands. Time after time these had failed to provide the security and safety that was needed. With nowhere else to turn, the Psalmist had discovered the security and safety of God's love.

For the Psalmist, and the people who read the Psalms, it was possible to be totally up front with God and tell him exactly how they felt. There was no need to be polite, speak in a posh voice using redundant words or get all religious and perform boring ceremonies. This wasn't an example of blind faith, a sort of 'when all else fails' type of thing. God had proved his love time and time again. God could be relied upon to keep his promises.

Just as all the emotions expressed in the Psalms are no different to what we feel now, God's love hasn't changed either. No matter how we feel, we can chat to God in the confidence that he won't reject us or go to sleep as we talk. It's not a case of '*when* all else fails' but '*before* all else fails', have a chat with God.

Ask each member of the group to take their piece of paper from the arrow-shaped sheet. Take a look at Psalm 62:8. Suggest that they rewrite verse 8, putting their own name before the verse and making the verse personal to them. For example: 'David, trust God, my friend, and always tell him each one of your concerns. God is your place of safety.'

(Allow 5 minutes.)

Ask the group to hold their piece of paper in their cupped hands while you read the following prayer:

Lord,
you may understand –
but I certainly don't –
why things happen to me
the way they do.
At times I feel like a magnet
that attracts
problems looking for a home.
Sometimes
I go to sleep feeling on top of the world
and wake up the next morning
with a head
that feels as if it's just been trampled on
by a herd of cattle.
Also, you may have noticed,
I've developed a bit of a stoop when I walk.
Having the weight of the world
on my shoulders
is a bit much for anyone to bear.
I've been let down, put down,
ignored and rejected.
But rather
than place my trust
in anyone
or any system
that will only make me feel
more screwed up than I am already,
I'm turning to you,
with all my baggage
and dodgy ways –
because you don't seem to care
that I'm not a neat, sorted, top-notch
kind of person –
you love me just the way I am.

BIBLE READING AND TOPIC INDEX

YEAR C

ADVENT

Unit 1	First Sunday of Advent	Luke 21:25-36	Christ's return
Unit 2	Second Sunday of Advent	Luke 3:1-6	Freedom
Unit 3	Third Sunday of Advent	Luke 3:7-18	Good news
Unit 4	Fourth Sunday of Advent	Luke 1:39-45	Trusting God

CHRISTMAS

Unit 5	First Sunday of Christmas	Luke 2:41-52	Perseverance
Unit 6	Second Sunday of Christmas	John 1:10-18	Friendship

EPIPHANY

Unit 7	The Epiphany	Matthew 2:1-12	Worship
Unit 8	First Sunday of Epiphany	Luke 3:15-17, 21-22	Baptism
Unit 9	Second Sunday of Epiphany	John 2:1-11	Miracles
Unit 10	Third Sunday of Epiphany	Luke 4:14-21	Freedom
Unit 11	Fourth Sunday of Epiphany	Luke 2:22-40	Trust

ORDINARY TIME

Unit 12	Proper 1	Luke 5:1-11	Miracles
Unit 13	Proper 2	Luke 6:17-26	Following God
Unit 14	Proper 3	Luke 6:27-38	Obedience

LENT

Unit 15	Second Sunday before Lent	Luke 8:22-25	Fear
Unit 16	Sunday next before Lent	Luke 9:28-36, 37-43	Authority
Unit 17	First Sunday of Lent	Luke 4:1-13	Confidence
Unit 18	Second Sunday of Lent	Luke 13:31-35	Obedience
Unit 19	Third Sunday of Lent	Luke 13:1-9	Forgiveness
Unit 20	Fourth Sunday of Lent	Luke 15:1-3, 11-32	Forgiveness
Unit 21	Fifth Sunday of Lent	John 12:1-8	Love
Unit 22	Palm Sunday	Luke 22:14-23	Communion

EASTER

Unit 23	Easter Sunday	Luke 24:1-12	Miracles
Unit 24	Second Sunday of Easter	John 20:19-31	Fear
Unit 25	Third Sunday of Easter	Acts 9:1-20	Friendship
Unit 26	Fourth Sunday of Easter	Acts 9:36-43	Death
Unit 27	Fifth Sunday of Easter	Acts 11:1-18	Acceptance
Unit 28	Sixth Sunday of Easter	Acts 16:9-15	Ambition
Unit 29	Seventh Sunday of Easter	Acts 16:16-34	Perseverance
Unit 30	Pentecost: Whit Sunday	Acts 2:1-21	Holy Spirit
Unit 31	Trinity Sunday	Romans 5:1-5	Perseverance

ORDINARY TIME

Unit 32		Galatians 1:1-12	Truth
Unit 33		Galatians 1:11-24	Acceptance
Unit 34		Galatians 2:(11-14), 15-21	Obedience
Unit 35		Galatians 3:23-29	Faith
Unit 36		Galatians 5:1, 13-25	Freedom
Unit 37		Galatians 6:(1-6), 7-16	Unselfishness
Unit 38		Colossians 1:1-14	Prayer
Unit 39		Colossians 1:15-28	God's love
Unit 40		Colossians 2:6-15	Trust
Unit 41		Colossians 3:1-11	Faith
Unit 42		Hebrews 11:1-3, 8-16	Trust
Unit 43		Psalm 80:1-2, 8-19	God's love
Unit 44	All Saints' Day	Psalm 149	Acceptance
Unit 45	Fourth Sunday before Advent	Psalm 32:1-7	Forgiveness
Unit 46	Third Sunday before Advent	Psalm 17:1-9	Honesty
Unit 47	Second Sunday before Advent	Psalm 98	Faith
Unit 48	Christ the King	Psalm 46	Worry

SCRIPTURAL INDEX

THEMATIC INDEX

SIDE ORDERS

The Internet is a mine of information. The main problem is that it can take a really long time to dig the information out! Not only that, it can become all too easy to feel as if you're stomping around in the dark.

To help you find your way around and avoid too much frustration, I have listed a selection of websites which will provide you with information and resources to accompany most of the units contained in this book.

Please note that although these websites were current at the time of writing, this doesn't mean that they will remain current or active. If you cannot locate a website, use one of the many search engines to find a site with a similar theme or topic.

BIBLE STUDIES
www.christianorigins.org (resources for the New Testament)
hometown.aol/wardfreman (UK secondary schools religious education topics)
http://www.fremancollege.herts.sch.uk/fremancollege/ (UK secondary schools religious education topics)

CHAT ROOMS
www.botcw.com (chat and articles)
www.cchat.net (a friendly voice)
www.circanet.org/ (chat rooms galore)

DRAMA
www.theworship.com/scripts/ (sketches)
www.drama4church.com (sketches for services)

EVANGELISM
www.alpha.org.uk (introduction to Christian faith)
www.christiananswers.net (offers answers to contemporary questions)
home.pix.za/gc/gc12/ (research and discussion)

HUMOUR
www.webcom.com/~ctt/comic.html (lots of fun stuff)
www.ship-of-fools.com (enter if you dare!)
www.quoteland.com (quotes!)

MAGAZINES
www.christianity.net/bc (a Christian perspective on key issues)
www.youthwork.co.uk (articles and resources)

MUSIC AND WORSHIP
www.cmo.com (info on Christian music scene)
www.christianbest.com/ (music resources)
www.crossrhythms.co.uk (news and reviews of Christian music)
www.praise.net/ (praise and worship)

SIDE ORDERS

NEWS
www.christiandailynews.org (wide-ranging news-site)
www.churchtimes.co.uk (Anglican weekly)

ORGANISATIONS
www.anglicansonline.org (Anglican news)
www.eauk.org (Evangelical Alliance)
www.wcc-coe.org (World Council of Churches)
www.iona.org.uk (Iona Community)

POLITICS
www.csworldwide.org/ (news on persecuted Christians)

SEARCH
www.jesus.org.uk/search/ (choose from main Christian directories)
www.allinone.org (compilation of Christian directories)
www.christiantopics.com (topic-based search engine)

YOUTH
www.careforce.co.uk (info on Christian volunteers)
www.cpas.org.uk (database of free resources)
www.christianteens.net/cyn/ (news)